MOHAWK

by Paul Fuhr
with Trasi Kromer

MOHAWK

Copyright © 2013 by Paul Fuhr.

All rights reserved. Printed in the United States of America. No part of this work may be reproduced or transmitted in any form or by any means, electronic or mechanical, including photocopying and recording, or by any information storage or retrieval system without the prior written permission of the copyright owner(s).

Cover art designed by Darren Simoes. Copyright © 2013.
Cover photography by Trasi Kromer. Copyright © 2012.

ISBN 978-1-300-48847-7

Published by Paradigm Press

Printed in the United States of America

1 2

Much love and many thanks to my family.

Also, for anyone and everyone who expected to see their name in this book: you aren't forgotten.

I can't tell every story.

- Shawn Daley

"BANG AND BLAME"
—R.E.M.

It wasn't even ten o'clock yet. The Hawaii air was thick and muggy, with a black canvas of bright stars arching high above me. My Marine squad leader Richard McCorkle (we called him "Big Dick") was supposed to meet me down at Waikíkí Beach to grab a few drinks.

For whatever reason, Big Dick didn't make it down. I didn't have a cell phone so I'm hitting pay phones left and right trying to find the guy.

I eventually thought *Screw this,* because I'm sure as shit not going to sit around all night drinking my face off—especially by myself.

I hailed a cab.

The main highway is straight in Honolulu, no curves, and both the exit-ramp and on-ramp are pretty damned close to one another. If someone would leave the exit-ramp and someone would enter the on-ramp at the same time, it was always a close call.

You could easily hit someone if you weren't paying attention.

And that's exactly what happened that night.

There was a girl riding a green Vespa—this beefy moped sort of thing—and she had no helmet on. She came tearing down the exit-ramp while someone was shooting up the on-ramp.

They took this poor girl out, throwing her completely off her bike.

My cab was probably five car lengths back when I saw this plume of white dust against the night sky. For some reason, I immediately knew what had happened. I didn't even think. I jumped out of the cab.

I don't know why; I just did.

The cab driver was yelling at me but I didn't care. I raced up the highway, full speed.

By the time I got there, her moped was still sliding across the asphalt. The girl had just stopped rolling. She looked so small on the ground, crumpled and bleeding bad. She'd been wearing nothing but a pair of shorts and a tank top. I was telling myself things like: *She could have a broken back. Don't move anything. Treat for shock.*

I have no idea where all of these thoughts were coming from, but they were coming fast and furious all the same.

People were standing around on the highway next to their cars, yelling: "What the hell's is going on?"

I was down next to her—trying to hold her legs up. She was completely unconscious, her hair going in every direction. There was blood everywhere and it looked black in the halogen lights.

Before I knew it, the two of us were completely surrounded. The few people who had those big-assed, bulky, flip cell phones weren't even calling for help. They were calling their friends and telling them what they're witnessing.

I finally screamed: *"Someone call 911!"*

I was trying to see if this girl was breathing, if she even had a pulse, and everyone was talking to other people on their phones.

The taxi driver, this Indian guy, caught up to me. He was all out of breath and pissed off. But when he finally saw what was going on, he didn't want any part of that shit. With one look, he shouted at me: *"Ah, you good! Don't worry about the car! You good, you good!"*

He was gone faster than he'd arrived, huffing it back down the embankment.

Finally, EMTs arrived. They all jumped out and got her stabilized. I rode with her in the back of the ambulance—this girl whose name I didn't even know.

I stayed at the hospital until somebody told me that The Girl Who Was In The Moped Accident was going to be okay.

I was covered in her blood but I didn't know who she was, and she didn't know me.

We'd never see each other again.

Maybe it was my Marine Corps training, maybe it was my instincts, maybe it was just me being me.

I don't know.

All I know is that I followed the same impulse I have with bad weather: everyone else goes to the basement while I go outside to see the storm.

I need to do that. Always.

> **"ALMOST CUT MY HAIR"**
> —Crosby, Stills, Nash & Young

My full name is Shawn Patrick Thomas Daley.

It's a tradition for Irish parents to throw an extra name onto the birth certificate during the baptism to honor a saint or someone they want being part of their child's spiritual life.

I was the first to get the extra middle name, but now you've got my nieces—Hannah Claire Montgomery Douglas and Ally Mackenzie Daley Douglas—sharing the tradition.

The proper Irish spelling of Shawn is "Sean" but Dad thought that was too stereotypical. Whatever that means. He liked "Shawn" because that's the Hebrew spelling and it translates to "the divine son of God," whereas "Sean" is Gaelic for "Jack." It's also because "Shawn" is my great uncle Jack and "Patrick" is my great uncle Pat. Thomas was my grandfather.

When it comes to royalty in Ireland, there are three families allowed to have yellow and red in their Coat of Arms: McCarthy, Daley, and O'Brien. The O'Briens were the last ruling family in Ireland and had the last king there. McCarthy and Daley were basically the support group for the O'Briens. The guardians.

The Daleys were the bards.

We were the poets, the singers, the performers for the king's court.

This explains pretty much everything you need to know about me.

I see music in colors and shapes. I can describe music as I'm listening to it, as I'm processing it, as a *thing*. I'm fascinated with music and genetics. I mean, are you born with a disposition to know what a Middle C is by hearing it in perfect pitch? Can you sit and tap your leg and maintain a tempo without speeding up or slowing down the beat in your head?

Is that genetic?

+

I'd always go to Irish festivals with my family but I never had a kilt. Growing up, nobody in my family did. Even the ones directly from Ireland couldn't afford a kilt. A true Irishman is not going to walk around with a kilt to know he's Irish.

That's the way I look at it—even though I own three kilts now.

Dad always says, "You should wear your kilt more" but I'm more of the "I don't need to wear it/What the hell is wrong with you?" mindset. I know I'm Irish. I've got ink on me that says so. I'm not too worried about wearing a kilt all the time to prove anything.

Still, I'm fascinated with the Irish. The stories, the lore, everything. St. Patrick, the patron saint of Ireland, wasn't even from Ireland. He was born in Scotland. He was brought to Ireland as a slave, escaped slavery, went back to Scotland, and became a minister.

He later became came a Catholic bishop and went back to "chase all the snakes out of Ireland," which amounted to him taking pagans and making them all Christian.

Did you know that the Celtic cross is a combination of the Catholic cross and the circle that the pagans used to symbolize unity? This dude combined the two and it's pretty fascinating that our model of religion still accepts that as okay—mainly because he was doing something like taking the Pentagram, the upside-down one with 666, and combining it with the Jewish Star.

It was like: "Dude, it's a great idea!"

And let's not forget traditions like the Cóiste Bodhar, which is Gaelic for "The Death Coach." The Irish don't fuck around, man. There's no St. Peter waiting at the gate to judge you.

When the Irish die—wherever you're at—nobody's allowed to be there with you.

When you're close to death, everyone leaves the room. No one sits there and holds your hand when you cross over. Your soul's supposed to be carried, alone, by this black carriage of four black horses and a scary dude with reins.

That's who judges you.

And that coach will take you to Heaven or it'll take you to Hell.

There's a story about my great-great aunt and my great-great grandmother that I love to tell. They were twins. The one twin died in 1918 in the influenza outbreak, and the other twin decided to stay in the room when her sister died.

Everyone else left the room and begged her to leave.

She refused.

The other twin said she saw the coach. She said she saw it all happen and that it was real.

If nothing else, it's a story that's passed down through my family and one I'll keep passing along.

+

I got to meet one of my namesakes, and I only met him once: my great uncle Pat.

He still had a thick Irish brogue.

He and my grandfather had a huge falling-out back in the 1930s over property in Vermilion, Ohio. Quarrel over a quarry.

So, my side of the family never got to socialize with Pat's kids or that side of the family. When Dad took me over to Pat's house when I was ten years old, it was literally like two months before the man died. I still remember hearing that very old, brittle, parchment-like voice.

This rift carried on for decades in the Daley family.

His kids—my cousins—were strangers to us. We never saw them. It was only a few years ago that we all agreed: "We need to stop this." I don't know who reached out to whom first, but our way of coming together was getting a tattoo.

A significant tattoo.

I knew exactly what we needed done. It was a pencil rubbing from a gravesite at a monastery in our hometown in Ireland. Dad had gone there and brought the rubbing home.

I e-mailed all of my cousins the rubbing and everyone loved it. So we all agreed to get the tattoo done at the same time.

It was in the basement of a biker bar—cobblestone walls plastered with mold. I was in this barber's chair out of the Fifties, and this dude named Tiny (who was not tiny) got it done for us.

My one cousin was still in his Army Reserve camouflage and we bonded.

We've been close ever since.

+

I can trace my family back, no shit, to 1139 A.D. Dead serious.

The recordkeeping in my family has always been pretty insane—passed down through family bibles. There wasn't Ancestry.com or anything to depend on.

I saw the actual place where my great-great-great grandfather, Patrick Henry Daley, stepped off the boat from Ireland into New York City. Right next door, I saw the place where he signed to become an American. And right next to *that* was the place where he signed to go to war.

Just like that. *Boom, boom, boom.*

He was paid one-hundred American dollars to take the place of a rich man from Connecticut in the Infantry unit for the Civil War. There was a table there when you got off the boat. He had his wife and five kids with him and he literally signed one ledger to become an American, then signed another to go to war.

They handed him one hundred dollars. He handed it to his wife and kids, got his uniform, and went off to war.

There was probably no better way to prove himself as an American than to die in that country for it. It's probably like joining a fraternity: you're going to be considered an outsider until you commit to it.

I have the actual roster that he signed, the roster of that unit with his name in it. His signature and a little star, which meant that he'd taken the place of somebody else that could afford to not fight.

He got wounded and put into reserves. That unit, turns out, was present at the signing of the Treaty at Appomattox Court House.

I have a thousand questions for this man:

Where the hell did the name "Henry" come from?

You were eighty when you died. How did you outlive everyone at the time? I mean, you literally blew the back wall out on life expectancy.[1]

You've got five kids. How did you think you'd survive?

Why did you come to America?

Why leave Ireland?

How did you choose between staying there and possibly starving, or coming here and possibly dying in a war?

Was it the hundred bucks?

---

[1] Especially when he was wounded in the Civil War.

"SUNSHINE SUPERMAN"
—Donovan

Dad flipped a coin to decide whether he became a musician or a minister.

I'm not joking. That's how he decided the course of his life. And ours, I guess.

The flip of a coin.

My father was on the road with a band—Alias Smith & Jones[2]—all through the Sixties. The funny thing about this was I didn't know my dad had been on the road or performed music until I was almost sixteen.

---

[2] The name comes from a Western TV series that aired on ABC.

Dad graduated from high school in 1963. He was working at the Fruehauf Trailer Company and they went on strike and there was no way to make money to pay for the house and for the family. It was just him and Mom.

They'd just gotten married and he was going broke, fast. So when the company went on strike, Dad and his cousins decided to form a band, go out, and play cover tunes to survive.

He'd actually been thinking about going into theology and becoming a minister. His mom was German; his dad was Irish. My grandfather gave up being a Catholic for his wife. I never got to know them.

I was born in the Blizzard of 1977—this brutal Lake Erie storm that was one for the history books. Sixty MPH wind gusts, huge piles of snow, no power. My grandfather froze to death in it. He'd gone out to stoke the fire—they had a wood burner in the garage—and he never came back in.

He was 77 years old in '77.

My family thinks he tripped and fell and froze to death. We'll never know.

My sister Christina always talked about spending the night over there. My grandparents had this big TV with giant rabbit-ear antennas and at two in the morning, there'd be this big Catholic mass on, just barely coming in through a haze of static.

She would catch our grandfather watching the Catholic mass, all washed out. That was the one piece of his past he had left: watching mass on TV at two in the morning. Once you leave Catholicism, the Catholics don't want you back. It's a pretty big deal. They don't forget, they don't forgive. So, he raised my father, my uncle, and my aunt as Lutheran.

Anyway, with the flip of a coin, Dad went on the path of becoming a musician. He went out on the road with this old school bus they'd converted into a tour vehicle. They went out on tour playing covers all the way from Vermont to Michigan and down along the East Coast.

There weren't any computers, no Internet, no actual books with chords and stuff in them to know what the newest hits on the radio were. You really had to stay on top of them.

That was Mom's job.

My mom and the wives of the other band members would sit in the kitchen on Saturday nights and listen to Dick Clark's *American Top 40* on the radio. One would sit there and scribble down the verses of the brand-new hits while another would be tasked with the chord progressions.

When the band came home once a month, they'd be issued handwritten "cheat sheets" to take back out on the road.

It was the late Sixties, probably '69, and they did this grand opening of a hotel in Aurora, right outside of Chicago. They co-headlined the opening of the hotel with Three Dog Night. (You know them: "Mama Told Me Not to Come," "One," and "Joy to the World.")

There's actually an archway in that hotel where everyone who performed that night signed the wood and they varnished it. Dad's autograph is still up there.

Christina used to fall asleep in the kick drum when they came home to practice. My sister has permanent loss of hearing in one ear because of that. When Dad was home, he wasn't there for my sister to sit on his lap and watch

TV. When they came home from the road, they did dry-cleaning and rehearsed.

That was it.

Their dry-cleaning bill on a monthly basis was about a thousand bucks. In 1969 dollars.

Dad played with Crosby, Nash and Young and got to go to Woodstock. He played the keyboard and when I say he played the keyboard, he fucking *played* it.

If Dad hears a song—just once—he can play it back to you. He can play the guitar part on his right hand and the bass guitar stuff with his left hand. He's a damned savant. He plays golf left-handed, writes right-handed, and does all these weird tricks on the piano with both hands.

In 1973, Alias Smith & Jones was getting ready to write an album. For the first time, they were going to do original music. Anyway, my dad's aunt was on her deathbed and Dad promised her—*promised*—that he'd become a father instead of somebody who came home once a month.

And he quit. Just like that.

This is the guy who owned *two* Leslie speakers. They're basically these huge—I mean *huge*—pieces of cabinetry with rotating speakers inside. You can't replicate the sound because it pretty much uses the Doppler Effect. You know that weird guitar part in U2's "One"? That's a Leslie right here.

My dad sold one of them for a down payment on my parents' first house.

+

At family Christmas parties, there was this incredibly out-of-tune Baby Grand piano and everyone would get Dad all liquored up so he'd screw around on it.

He could play it blindfolded and backwards. He'd play it frontwards, then spin around and play it behind his back. They'd do sing-a-longs and shit. That was all I knew about Dad's music abilities at the time: watching him "play" at Christmas.

His piano teacher actually got committed to a mental institution. No joke. I'm not sure the two things were related, but it got to a point where my dad was outplaying her at a really young age.

When I started seriously getting interested in music, I was thirteen and I'd gotten my first bass guitar in my hands. I'd sit down and we'd play Christmas songs together: "Greensleeves," "What Child Is This?" And what's crazy is that I had a bass guitar teacher who was really adamant about how I tuned. You know, just like a nun cracking you on the knuckles if you didn't do something right.

I'd always be completely in tune but Dad's piano would be way out of whack. So, I'd have to de-tune my bass to his piano in order to play together. We'd play for hours, crazily out of tune, but it didn't matter.

I loved it. It felt normal.

It was like *Leave It To Beaver* in my house. At least that's what Dad wanted it to be. The problem is that a large part of him couldn't really, in good conscience, conform to it.

"FADE INTO YOU"
—Mazzy Star

Downtown Milan, Ohio is a collection of dusty antique shops, a couple of family restaurants, City Hall, a library, a funeral home, and a couple of churches surrounding a modest town square. There's one drive-thru, one gas station, and one stop light. Jim's Pizza Box. The Invention. Crosby's Antiques. Sipe's Hair Shop. The Wonder Bar and the Park Lounge.[3]

Everything you need from a small town.

---

[3] Back in the day, there used to be a goddamned *gunstore* between these two bars.

It's also the birthplace of Thomas Edison. Don't forget that. Milan's been riding on that nugget for ages.

There also used to be a restaurant on the town square called Grundy's Loft. Restaurant downstairs, bar upstairs. I forget the name of the bar, but Grundy's was a Milan landmark.

Well, one afternoon while they were doing remodeling in there, someone removed the main support beam. Next thing you know, the whole restaurant started to sink down under its own weight. Now, mind you, Grundy's wasn't its own place—it's right in the center of this one, long brick building that it shares with a realty office, an antique shop, and a flea market.

The fire and police departments from Norwalk, one town over, had to come in. Milan didn't have a big enough ladder truck to get over Grundy's to check on the damage.

Turns out, natural gas was leaking out and the firefighters and the police and the city officials were all scrambling to figure out how to shut down the gas leak and somehow keep this building from crumbling out into the street.

Before you knew it, two hundred, maybe two hundred-fifty people were out in the square, sitting on folding chairs and watching the world's slowest demolition job ever on a Friday night.

Everyone was ordered not to smoke because of the natural gas—and my mom was a smoker back then, so she wasn't really interested in seeing Grundy's come down. If there had been an explosion, it would've taken out the entire town square. I'm serious. Dick Smith Realty probably would've been launched into space.

When it got dark, they threw these searchlights up on the building like there was a goddamned loose gorilla up there or something. I remember looking around at everyone watching Grundy's slowly coming down and being pissed that I didn't have a hot dog cart. I would've made a mint.

I kept thinking someone's gotta get soda pop cans up there, man. Some hamburgers. Popcorn. Something. We're all camping out and we're seeing this thing through.

We're all gonna watch Grundy's come down.

As a town.

Together.

That's Milan, Ohio in a nutshell: Two hundred people sharing the experience of watching their beloved restaurant, this local landmark, come down at a snail's pace all through the night.

+

Milan's the same now as it was when I was growing up there which is part of its charm, I guess. It's a very conservative, New England-ish community that's as safe as it is protective of the people who live there.

Whenever I think of Milan, I always imagine it as though it's the small-town backdrop of a movie taking place during Halloween.

I remember back when there was a general store and there were old geezers sitting out front playing chess. In my mind it's always autumn there, with scarlet leaves scuttling down the sidewalks and bare trees rustling in the wind. There's a big clock tower that keeps a dark watch over everything at night and there's a creepy cemetery with weathered monuments and ivy-covered mausoleums.

Everyone knows each other in Milan. There's no way in hell you can keep a secret. No way. Growing up, there was this old 1940s air-raid siren that the Fire Department cranked up for emergencies and it'd send this chilling wail throughout the town.

I'm sure the phone company's circuit board lit up like a Christmas tree whenever that thing went off.

Everyone would be calling everyone else asking: "Where's the fire at? What's going on?" We kicked things up a notch in my family by getting a police scanner. When that siren went off, we'd gather around the scanner like a hobo barrel fire, listening to what was happening a few streets over or somewhere out in the country.

We always knew what was going on.

My mom worked at Eastman's, the local grocery store, which lasted for years and years until Meijer and Wal-Mart moved in. My dad was a city councilman. My sister's ten years old than me and she was a cheerleader.

Talk about quintessential small-town America.

+

The streets would be crammed with ramshackle fair-circuit rides—Tilt-a-Whirl, sky swing, bumper cars—and there was always a bingo game going on in the town hall. The air was always thick and heavy with the smell of funnel cakes and the sounds of life.

Milan came alive over Labor Day weekend in the way all small towns do when it's their annual moment to shine. Labor Day weekend is when the Melon Festival began.[4]

Rain or shine, it's the one institution that we had. Thousands of people descended upon the tiny town square from all over the state, lumbering through Milan and squeezing through the narrow pathways that cut between hamburger stands, sausage stands, and ice cream booths.[5]

It's where everyone came home from all walks of life, from all over. And if people weren't home, they were wishing they were. I mean, I couldn't wait to get the hell out of Milan and all of our friends said the same. There's no way they'd ever come back to this burned-out little hole-in-the-wall town.

Fuck this, man. I'm Doc Hollywood. I'm out!

---

[4] We had a "Melon Queen" every year. Yes, you read that right.
[5] Words cannot describe how excited people got over melon ice cream—and how upset they got when it was sold out.

But *everyone* I talk to—even the hardest of the hard—*always* ask about the Melon Festival every year. It's always: "Did you see so-and-so?" and "What went on?" and "Who was at the beer tent?" It's never: "Screw that place, man."

The Melon Festival is an institution.

The parade. The fire trucks. The marching band. Some of the most indelible memories I have in life are Jolly Ranchers being thrown at my head at the speed of light and the smell of the firemen's BBQ.

"SHE SELLS SANCTUARY"
—The Cult

I still can't think about parent-teacher conferences without getting sick to my stomach—and I'm in my thirties.

I always had slips from my teachers disciplining me for talking in class or some shit. Every time, I had to take the slip home for Mom to sign and then bring it back to show that she knew what was going on at school.

Well, what I would do is have Mom sit down and practice her signature with me as I was "practicing" mine to improve myself. Then, I would take her scrap copies of paper and transfer them over to the slips.

I got away with that for an entire school year.

The next year? I got hit.

Mom went to school for a parent-teacher conference and I was at home. I was so nervous the whole time she was gone that I was pacing the house, telling myself she wouldn't figure out what I'd been doing.

She was handed all of these slips that she'd supposedly signed, saying she was already aware that I was flunking this, failing that, had interrupted this class, had not turned in some piece of homework.

Mom came home and she was infuriated. Most of all, I think she was embarrassed.

It killed me.

That night, Dad instructed me to get my own branch from the apple tree. You're reading that correctly. It's not a metaphor. He literally made me go out back and cut down a branch from the apple tree, then meet him in the attic above the garage for a whipping.

The next day at school, it was the teachers' turn.

I got paddled by the principal Mrs. Williams, this slight lady, in her office. Back then, you could get away with that shit. Honestly, though, she was one hell of a lame paddler.

There was nothing behind it.

Then again, after Dad, I'm pretty sure I wouldn't have been able to feel anything.

+

Mom had been an intern for President Lyndon B. Johnson. She still talks about it today. Mom actually got a necklace from Johnson on her birthday. We were robbed one year and it was stolen with a bunch of Dad's guns. She was so torn up about losing that necklace, but she still has this little elephant ornament from Johnson.

I don't know how she got the job, but she lived in D.C. with her mom and aunt, who were hairdressers at the time. All I know is that she loved that job. They even evacuated the city when the city burned down in the riots of 1968. All three of them stood up on the same hill from the 1812 burning.

+

Halloween is huge for me and Mom.

It started off with me being a dragon for Halloween. The dragon was basically this skeleton made out of PVC pipe. Mom overlaid it with foam rubber and painted on the scales. It was built to sit on my shoulders and be balanced. This thing had to have been twelve feet long and ten feet tall. My sister was Guinevere and she led me around the damn school.

Thanks to Mom, I won every Halloween contest, every year.

One year, I was the character from *Re-Animator*, the mad scientist who comes back from the dead. I carried my own head.

I was a werewolf. I was a ghost. Vlad from *Dracula*. One year, I was Merlin. For that, we took the *Re-Animator* costume, so it was Merlin carrying his globe (my head) around.

Recently even, Mom made me a full red sequined tux. I dyed my hair the color of a yellow flashlight, spiked it all out, and put in semi-permanent fangs.

I was a very *fabulous* devil.

+

Mom was the den leader of a Girl Scout troop and I was pretty much their mascot. It was around maybe 1983 and I was five years old.

One of the main memories I have is them getting into shaving cream fights at camp. While I'm sitting there watching them run around, I'd get *thwapped* in the face with shaving cream as they went past me. About ten minutes would go by and I'd be completely covered in it.

I didn't have the strength in my fingers and hands yet to make a can of shaving cream do a damn thing.

I couldn't fight back.

I started crying my eyes out because I was just covered in that shit. Everyone's laughing and giggling and then they figure out why I'm bawling and each one of them came over to kneel down beside me.

They gave me a can.

I had to use my whole fist and every ounce of strength to shoot anything out of it. They'd run over and let me shoot something on their foot or knee.

I was still crying.

+

Mom is notorious with her predictions. She sees things happen before they happen. To this day, if she sees me doing something or getting ready to go somewhere, sometimes she'll have me sit down and have a cup of coffee or something. It's like she's slowing me down—in a good way.

When I was young, she'd sometimes say: "I need you to sit down for ten minutes before you can go anywhere."

Sure as shit, a semi would take out a car on the road I was going to drive on. She's done this with Dad; she's even done this during my deployments in the Marines.

She senses things you can't teach.

Sometimes it's good, sometimes it's horrible.

I don't like knowing something is about to happen. Especially if it's bad. Just let it happen and let it happen quick.

Mom has always seemed to know what's lurking just around the corner.

"WELCOME TO THIS WORLD"
—Primus

When Gundy's Loft collapsed in the middle of the night, it couldn't possibly kill what it'd started. It was the birthplace of the first-ever Edison High School show choir.

There was this group of high schoolers who worked there on Wednesday nights as singing waiters and waitresses. Every hour on the half-hour mark, they'd do a show with the upright piano there. Kevin Kiser would play it and they'd all just work for tips.

I was six years old the very first time I saw them perform. I just remember watching them in awe: these high schoolers, singing while they were working. They were an elite unit, a well-oiled machine singing "You're the One That I Want" from *Grease* and songs from *My Fair Lady*. And they did a lot of their own writing, too. There was a musical called *Don't Drink the Water* that I'm pretty sure they wrote.

It was all I needed to see. I was hooked.

+

In elementary school, I had two musical choices: tonette band or choir. I chose choir because there's no way in hell I was going to play a freaking plastic recorder.

The tonette is a flute-like instrument played through a reed. In other words, it's a well-tuned kazoo.

I don't know how or why you would ever create a band with tonettes. It was ridiculous. It was like something you'd get out of a Cracker Jack box, but Milan Elementary had an entire "band" made up of these things.

I like to think it's something along the lines of a bad bet. If you lost, you played tonette.

Then again, choosing choir over tonette band meant having to spend time with Mrs. Wargo—this older, creepy woman who'd make you sit on her knee as the class sang you "Happy Birthday," all while she's pinching your ass. I'm not joking. We're seven years old, mind you, and she's pinching our asses.

That shit wasn't right.

+

In fifth grade, I rocked my first mohawk. We did this concert that was music all through the ages or something—songs from every era—and we ended up doing something futuristic at the end.

We had all these strobe lights and it was *Star Trek*-themed, I think. We didn't sing anything but I remember it being highly choreographed: Jayne Miller, Kim Ball, Matt Heid, Nate Jennings—all of us out there in the dark, strobes going off, the girls slinking around in the dark in black leotards. Electronic music pulsing in the background.

It was trippy, man. Especially for a fifth grader.

What the hell were they thinking?

+

It's important to have your own music when you're growing up. And it's even more important for that music to change and grow with you.

When I was younger, it was my chance to jump on a bandwagon that nobody else ever had before. I was learning about bands right as they rolled out: Pearl Jam, Nirvana, Pixies, Jane's Addiction, Porno for Pyros, Primus.

For every new genre that comes out, I'm morbidly curious. Shoegaze, trip-hop, lo-fi garage rock. Even this whole folk revival that's going on right now reminds me that it's all circular. Look at the big band, swing music revival in the 1990s—that Zoot Suit Riot, Brian Setzer Orchestra sort of thing. I think it fit that decade to a "T" and says a lot about the era from which it came.

I'm wondering what our music now will say about us later. But that's the whole point of music. It's about the "now"—not how it's going to look and feel and sound years from now. You can't possibly ever know that.

+

Freshman year, 1991. Edison High School. That's when that grunge music was all over MTV and the radio.

Oversized flannel lumberjack shirts, sad faces, stuff like that. Pearl Jam's "Jeremy" video, the one where the angry kid shoots up a classroom. Metallica's black-and-white "Enter Sandman." Nirvana's "Smells Like Teen Spirit"? Hell, I could practically feel the sweat and the grime of that video coming off the screen. What's more is that I *understood* what they were commenting on.

Those videos are iconic now.

I started hearing bands like that—Alice and Chains, Soundgarden—on 89X out of Detroit while getting rides home from Todd Koch, Steve Weit, and Christine Kubeck. I started hearing the stuff they were listening to.

There's a lot to be said about that period in your life when you're so young and so impressionable about everything. Music has a way of finding its way into you easier than other things. And it helps that everything at that age maybe cuts closer to the bone and everything sinks in a little deeper than when you're older.

You'll never forget where you were when you first heard Crazy Different Music No One's Ever Heard Before.

Before that, I wasn't really a fan of Guns 'n Roses or those hair bands you probably think I'm a fan of. No, I was listening to Prince and the New Power Generation, Paula Abdul, and Taylor Dayne.

#truestory.

I'd grown up on the Beach Boys. Crosby, Stills, Nash & Young. The Eagles. There's an audio recording of me singing "All the Gold in California" by the Gatlin Brothers somewhere out there. (That was huge when I was six, let me tell you.)

I was heavily influenced by anything and everything around me, so having a sister who was huge into Prince, Apollonia, and Morris Day and the Time couldn't have affected me more.

With Mom and Dad working all the time, that's all I heard in my house: fucking *Purple Rain*.

+

When I turned fourteen, I felt everyone on the planet was playing guitar or learning how to play the guitar. I thought it'd be a good idea to try to be that one dude everyone needed.

I instantly thought: *No one's playing bass.*

So I figured if I played the one instrument nobody else was, I'd always be busy and I'd always be playing. And I was. I could pick and choose who I wanted to play with because I was the only one playing bass.

I started playing anywhere I could: with stage bands, with friends in basements. It didn't matter. In 1992, I decided that without any real training or practice, it'd be smart to go for broke with the high school talent show.

I gathered a few people together and we chose Pearl Jam's "Alive," which was huge at the time.

I remember sitting at Mike Prout's house, though I can't remember why. Maybe it was because he had a drum set and I didn't. Mike was this skinny, explosive, highly intelligent dude who loved doing impressions of Jim Carrey as Ace Ventura, Pet Detective. I remember we were in some back room that Mike's mom has since turned into a bedroom, going over and over and over that damned song.

Mike could never stand and play guitar at the same time. He had to sit and play as if he were learning. He was always an eager guy, though. He wanted to get it right.

I was (of course) on bass.

Mike was just learning rhythm guitar and barely rhythm at that. He was playing these simple riffs you get out of a book. None of it was coordinated, but I remember his guitar: a brand-new, seafoam green Fender.[6]

It's me, Mike, Steve Lener and Matt Raymond all in this room. Steve's a perfectionist with a giant noggin[7] and someone who loved sporting skater shirts. Matt was this guy with shaggy hair, flannel shirts, and farmer's hands. He was also the shiest lead singer you've ever seen. Matt couldn't make eye contact with anything except the floor.

Steve was on drums but had to keep stopping to show Mike how to play things on the guitar, then jump back behind the drum kit. Matt was singing and every once in a while, Mike's dad would come in with a tambourine.

We spent so much time working on that song for the talent show and, in the end, we never even did it.

---

[6] Brad Bailey ended up buying that guitar by the way, and I'm still trying to hunt it down.
[7] Seriously: his head is huge.

We ended up playing "Creep" by Stone Temple Pilots, which we practiced maybe twice. Needless to say, we didn't win. I don't even think we got an award for showing up.

But I was finally playing music with friends and looking at doing shows. And during those days it was *so* important to me to have a show to play. Everyone else was happy just playing in the basement but that wasn't enough.

I wanted to win that goddamned talent show.

I wanted to prove ourselves as musicians. There weren't any delusions about signing to a label, nothing like that. I just wanted to get better and it was more about just being in a band—any band—than anything else.

My basement became Ground Zero for people to come and play music. I remember Dan Haas was on drums at one point; Brad Bailey played guitar. People moved around, in and out. Steve played guitar but he spent more time fucking around with a video camera and documenting everything than being part of the music.

I'll be honest: it was pretty critical to get airbrushed T-shirts at the Sandusky Mall with our band name "Spark"[8]

---

[8] The band name came from Phil Weilnau's dad "Sparky," who had a piece of wood with *SPARK* carved into it.

on it. And we got those done. That was Priority One for a while. I was so pissed, though, because Matt Raymond immediately gave his shirt to some chick at 4H camp. I was like: "You son of a bitch."

I don't know where my mine went but I can guarantee there isn't one anywhere now.

+

Tom Schenk used to make me memorize Primus songs in my attic above the garage. I'd being learning those thick, swampy, bass-driven songs and he'd be saying, "Play that again" or "You missed a note there" or "No, play that again." And I'd do it. We'd sit up there drinking warm Pepsis out of those old glass bottles.

The attic was this damp, old, open space with a fine layer of dust over everything. There were cobwebs in the corners, Christmas ornaments from the 1930s, an old cast iron sewing machine, my Tonka toys, and my sister's old Barbie dolls. Miscellaneous furniture scattered everywhere. Things that families tend to hold onto and never let go, like a Christmas tree made entirely out of garland. It looked like something out of a 1950s space flick.

Tom and I would be up there for hours, trying to connect as many speakers as we could get our hands on to one amplifier to make it louder. We thought that would make it louder. We understood Ohm's Law[9] and all that happy horseshit, but we just wanted to make it *loud*.

So, we would just hook up all kinds of speakers and blast Primus and weird stuff like They Might Be Giants. I'd memorize everything. I was a machine. I remember all of "Istanbul" and all of its lyrics because of Tom Schenk.

Tom was one of the guys I knew a lot longer than most everyone else because our families were so close. We knew one another when we were five years old. We were in Cub Scouts together. His family would have us over for hog roasts and we'd all play and go swimming together.

I can't quite put my finger on how we went from average kids to crossing over into Oddville. Maybe it was the music. Who the hell knows? I just remember Tom wearing an Astros jersey all the time and using a bowling

---

[9] The current through a conductor between two points is directly proportional to the potential difference across the two points.

bag for a bookbag. He had a big messy mop of Tom Schenk hair. He was the original Napoleon Dynamite: awkward and weird and fun.

That dude mounted a record player in his Bronco. Read that sentence again. He had a 1978 Bronco that had a CD player in it, but that was too easy for Tom. So, he mounted a record player to play vinyl on the way to school.

That's the kind of guy I'm talking about.

+

I wrote the lyrics to a song of mine on the back of a sheet music jacket from concert band.

I accidentally left it on the band bus. Sophomore year. I came running back to the bus, and Mr. Georgiafandis had the folder in his hand.

Mr. Georgiafandis (or "Mr. G" as everyone called him) was the high school music director and, by all accounts, the highest-paid person at the school.

Mr. G was a stout man with a salt-and-pepper beard and this booming, tremulous voice. The dude wore black knee socks with shorts, but that was part of his charm. I think the man gained three decades of classes' trust and love and loyalty by allowing things to happen that would normally be frowned upon.

Let's talk about an unsanctioned school trip to Toronto.

No permission slips, no educational value, nothing. But somehow, we had school buses all the same. It was like Fight Club. We didn't talk about it. It just happened.

That's who Mr. G was.

Larger than life. Made shit happen.

Anyway, he asked me about the lyrics.

I told him what they meant. It was something along the lines of Nine Inch Nails' "Something That I Can Never Have." You know, me being an "oppressed teenager" and wishing I wasn't an awkward fuck who was into comic books and paintball and The Blues Brothers. Everyone else seemed to be having fun going to Homecoming dances and shit.

Not me. I didn't see a dance until my senior year.

But Mr. G liked my lyrics and it was the first time I felt validated. It wasn't just my friends and family. If you weren't good, Mr. G didn't have trouble telling you. If you were the squeaky wheel at band camp and didn't perform your part right, you'd run laps and rehearse until you *did* get it right. It happened to me all the time.

I sucked, so I spent a lot of band camp running around and playing tuba.

I can't describe the feeling of Mr. G telling me that something I wrote was actually good.

+

I first performed with my dad publicly during a high school band concert. It was in the spring and there was an intermission during the concert. They needed music to fill the gap, so Mrs. Reilly, the assistant music director, said: "Go ahead and do it if you and your dad want to."

We rehearsed for *weeks*. Dad would be on piano and I was playing bass and, somehow, Tom played drums. Never mind that Tom didn't actually play drums. Tom didn't play shit.

But there was Tom playing drums all the same.

I remember we had one rehearsal in my parents' basement and all of the sudden Tom showed up and he's playing drums to some CCR cover.

No one sang, either. That's the best part. We were essentially doing that old drive-in *Let's go down to the lobby, let's go down to the lobby, let's go down to the lobby, and get ourselves a drink!* That's what it was. We were the walking cartoon soda pops and hot dogs and popcorn bags.

Tom and I were so fucking nervous, it was hilarious. I remember shaking up there on the stage, trying to work through my nerves.

A decade later, I would be onstage in Detroit with an entirely different band, competing for a million dollars.

We were preparing to head to band camp for the last time and it was a tradition for Mr. G. to take the seniors the day before so we could get set up for the week and relax.

While most of the other seniors brought TVs, VCRs, fans, stereos—nothing too outrageous—Shawn ended up with his own room and unpacked a sousaphone, marching tuba, stereo, and an amplifier setup that was as tall as he was.

That's what I think of Shawn: "Go big or go home."

- Neal Doerner

"DREAM WEAVER"
—Gary Wright

We were all out there, taking the football field on a cold October night.

It was damp and barely forty degrees. We could see our breath exploding against the field lights. I always wanted to be in the marching band and now that I finally *was* in the marching band, I didn't want to be there.

The Edison High School marching band was no joke. It was renowned across the entire state. Hundreds of us, all wearing orange and blue.[10] The band was so big that there were actually cliqués within it. There were preppy kids, theater nuts, nerds.

It was surreal.

It was a big Homecoming game and when I ran out there, I was already out of breath. Back then, I smoked cigarettes and I was carrying a goddamned tuba over my head on the football field, looking like a fool.

It absolutely killed my back. Imagine growing up fourteen years of your life wanting to be in the band and now you don't want to be. You're proud of it, but you pass out afterward.[11]

I remember we got to walk down through the tunnel that night. It's a tradition at Edison that all the tuba players bow—big tuba bells down—to the senior tubas when they come walking by.

---

[10] Worst school color combination in history.

[11] The secret to being in Edison High School's marching band might really be getting a chiropractor, hitting up Dave's Drive-In out on Route 60, or smuggling in some Mad Dog 20/20.

It's moments like that that I really remember—not so much the agony of carrying a giant fucking tuba across a freezing field.

I also think of all of those moments *after* the games. Hanging out at Jim's Pizza Box. Heading out to Huron to the block house out on the lake with John, Steve, and Mike.

It wasn't so cool to hang out with your parents after a game anymore.

+

I wasn't that good at marching band. I wasn't First Chair—not even close. Try Fourth or Fifth Chair. And that's because a lot of it bored me. Learning Rachmaninoff or *M*A*S*H* on a tuba was not my idea of learning music.

I enjoy that stuff now but back then, I wanted my Nirvana and I wanted my Ministry. I wanted the cerebral side of it, not a medley of *Star Trek* theme songs. But everyone told me you've got to start at the bottom with music and learn your way up.

You can't shortcut the learning process with music.

+

When we traveled between schools, there was only one marching band bus (of the five) to be on.

Mine.

I was always in the back of the bus with the loudest boom box of everyone. It was a Sony and it took twelve D-cell batteries. It had a built-in CD player—this push-top bubble—with two detachable side speakers. One person held a speaker in one direction as someone else held the other in a different one.

On the way to every football game, it became a tradition. I'd have the boom box on my lap and people would start winging CD cases at me.

We'd play everything from The Doors to The Jesus and Mary Chain to R.E.M. It was the first time I deejayed. All I wanted was to keep the energy high.

It was loud, it was fun, it was all about singing along to music that was our parents'. A lot of it was our music, though: Stone Temple Pilots, Bush, Presidents of the United States of America.

The back seven rows of that bus would be a big party.

We always begged for chaperones who'd be cool with it. Sometimes we'd get a little rowdy and hear from the front: *"Cool it off back there!"* We'd quiet down and then play a song mocking them.

Whenever someone yelled at us to calm the fuck down, we'd put on "Enjoy the Silence" by Depeche Mode.

+

Band camp on Kelley's Island was hot, humid, and smelled of rotting fish. I shared a cabin with Jon Caskey, Tom Schenk, Steve Lener, and Joe Valez. Caskey had been this tiny guy for as long as I could remember and then, one summer, he turned into the Jolly Green Giant, tying his long hair up with a rubber band.

Valez was a different story. He was this quiet, dark, puzzling dude who you could never quite get a read on. He didn't emote. You never knew if he was sad, happy, or solving a math problem in his head.

You could give that guy a million dollars and he'd just stare at it, dead-eyed.

Anyway, I had a pair of handcuffs on me. Real handcuffs. (Don't ask.) We were getting ready to meet out in the field to do exercises one morning and Valez was taking his sweet time.

He didn't want to get out of his rack. I go: "I'm going to handcuff you to the rack if you don't get your ass out of there."

Jon and Tom were all like: "You ain't got the balls, Daley."

So I literally reached over and handcuffed Valez to his rack.

I didn't have a key, so we did the only thing that made sense: we all ran out the door.

That guy was handcuffed there for probably a good hour or two. He's there yelling and no one can hear him because we're all out on the field marching.

"Where's Valdez?" someone would demand, and we'd all shrug.

They had to get the maintenance guy to get lock cutters.

+

There was a tradition that had started in the early Eighties. If you were a senior, you picked a freshman and that person was your "slave." They basically helped clean your cabin and do various other tasks like getting food and carrying instruments. It was demeaning, but a rite of passage.

I was a slave for Vicki Wick. She was fucking brutal. I remember Vicki having big hair and a big personality. We're friends now, but *goddamn*. She wanted things done in an exact way. Every morning, I had to go in and clean their cabin. I once had to race someone else by rolling a hot dog across the room with my nose.

It was very important that we kept that slave thing going. (Mainly because, years later, I was going to make someone else pay for this nonsense.) It was brutal and it went on all week but, by the end of the week, I was relieved of slave duty and considered somewhat of an equal. (Which is to say I was not treated like shit anymore.)

Anyway, when I was a senior, I didn't get a slave.

Nope.

No one did.

Thanks to a cease-and-desist letter from a freshman's mom who was a lawyer, twenty years of a tradition came to a screeching halt. That kid simply didn't want to be a slave, simply didn't want to be part of the process. End of story. One letter and the entire tradition was gone.

I'd been treated like shit for nothing.

For some unknown reason, Daley and I fought at least two or three times in school. I still have no idea why. What I remember of the fights is pretty sad, too. I believe we scuffled behind a church in Milan, in his driveway, and maybe once in the locker room.

The only detail I remember of any of them is Daley at one point swinging from a clothesline—totally bad-ass ninja style—and kicking me. I really have no clue why we fought and to this day, I feel bad about it and wish it had never happened.

We are much better friends than we were pugilists. I love that guy like a brother. One of the most positive, kindest and most compassionate people the world will ever know.

- Cory Roberts

"COME AS YOU ARE"
—Nirvana

In high school, I had a 1978 Jeep Wrangler. All beat to hell. The back seat wasn't bolted down and I had these stolen traffic signs for a floor.

I could make it backfire on command. It was beautiful.

Whenever I'd shift from fourth gear down to third gear, then creep her into second, I could make everyone in a quarter-mile scatter.

One night after a football game, I was facing the only traffic light in town. The gas station was on the left and the funeral home was on the right. And out of Jim's Pizza Box comes the entire girl's volleyball team. Without warning, they all jump onto—and into—the Jeep.

There's about eight or ten of them, all glommed onto my Jeep like zebra mussels or something. I kept yelling: *"I'm going to get into trouble! I'm going to get into trouble!"*

I remember Jayne Miller telling me: "We just want to go around the block."

I made it to the corner, maybe twenty feet, and instantly got pulled over. Milan PD. The girls took off in a thousand directions and I'm sitting there like an asshole.

The cop didn't ticket me or anything. He was actually laughing, looking at me like: "No way in hell did you just try that."

That's when I knew. Something happened there.

Lightning struck.

+

I was sitting in study hall, not studying and just doodling on my notebook. Second-to-last period. Mr. Welfle—this gargantuan, burly man—walked up from behind me, grabbed me by the scruff of my neck like a damn dog, and stood me up.

My chair squealed like hell and everyone turned around to look.

I'll never forget what he said.

"Everyone, please look at this person. Understand that he'll be serving you burgers after he gets done with high school."

I didn't even know the guy. He was the shop teacher, but I thought he was the janitor half the time. That moment honestly—to this day—still resonates with me and motivates me if I'm having a rough morning, if the stress is getting high, or if I'm just struggling to get by.

Here I was—me and this authority figure I don't even know—in front of my peers. People I've never even met, really, are being told what my outcome in life is going to be.

+

There weren't many groups or cliques in school. You had preps and jocks, sure, but there wasn't an Abercrombie & Fitch to feed them the clothes they needed back then. (Not in Northern Ohio, anyway.) It was more like polo shirts and jerseys for the Homecoming kings and queens.

One of my good friends in the popular crowd was Frank Carrico, the football quarterback. He looked the part, too: tall, thin, dark-haired, good cheekbones. And nobody actually knew that Frank went out of his way to hang out with people like me, Tom, and Jon.

If I'd accidentally run into a gaggle of football players at a party, they'd all go: "What the fuck is Daley doing here?" But Frank would be the first one to say: "Hey, hey, hey—he's with me."

I managed to get by on the gift of gab, talking about anything. I can relate to sports, sort of. I could pretend to know what you're talking about.

My parents had gotten me into martial arts at an early age and I advanced quickly. It was more than just a pastime—it was something I loved dearly. Took me ten years to go through ten different belts—all the way to black.

The training regime of martial arts helped me out with the football players, strangely enough. I found myself giving those dudes some techniques, training-wise, to get endurance: center of gravity stuff, attacking low, how to shift your weight to bring somebody down.

In all honesty, they were probably things football players couldn't even use. Still, they loved it and all of a sudden, I wasn't such an awkward asshole in their eyes.

+

I tried cross country in high school.

Once.

Ironically, this was on the urging of a big, angry woman I'll call "Mrs. H." She taught math and I'm pretty goddamned sure she didn't have a conscience.

One day, I ran out to her car to get her purse in the pouring rain. She timed me. For some reason, she was like: "You definitely need to go out for cross country."

I was floored.

Instead of suggesting I go run sprints for the track team, she was trying to put my ass into a five-mile run.

Simply because she was too large and lazy to get her purse in the rain.

It didn't matter. I believed her.

She bullied me into joining the cross country team. I was completely miserable. There was nothing fun or redeemable or interesting about it. Unlike martial arts, it wasn't me-versus-you. It was me-against-the-world and me-against-myself.

The team made fun of me so much because I couldn't run. I was horrible.

I still can't run.

+

If I had to sum up my high school experiences into one story, it'd be this one.

I was driving with Jimmy Boyce and Shawn Salmons after band practice, coming out of the field house. It was a quarter-mile stretch of road from the field house to the high school so, instead of jumping inside, I jumped onto the roof.

It made sense at the time.

My hands were around the doors because they were open. We were driving really slow down the road with the doors open, blasting Alice in Chains.

Shawn suddenly slammed his door shut.

My pinky finger was still in the door.

I'm screaming as we're driving down the road, smacking the roof as hard as I could.

I didn't realize that I was slamming it to the beat of the music. They thought I was just digging the music.

There we all were, casually creeping up the road with "Man in the Box" blasting from the speakers and my finger stuck in the door.

They finally pull up and turn the car off and I'm still screaming. Shawn opens up his door and I collapse onto the ground. He'd dislocated my finger.

I'm writhing around on the pavement, but they didn't know any better.

They couldn't distinguish me from the bass line, I guess.

I met Shawn when I was five years old. He chased me around my yard while our dads talked about something. I always felt welcome at the Daleys' house. He was always friendly and ready to party. When I think of Shawn, I think of all my friends being together, listening to loud Marilyn Manson or White Zombie in a crappy car, just goofing off. He was also a surprisingly good show choir partner.

- Melanie Lowey

"I ALONE"
—Live

Girls used to be elusive, to say the least.

I guess it started with Farrah Deitrich in third grade. I was chasing her around the playground right next to the jungle gym. She'd torn off her jacket and was swinging it all around to keep me away. Just when I was about to pounce and tackle her ass, Farrah whipped that jacket at me.

Turns out, there was a rock in one of the pockets.

She David-and-Goliath'd me right down to the ground.

For some reason, I blamed Rachel Blakeman for it. They even brought that poor girl in. I was like: *"You did this! YOU DID THIS!"*

Farrah owned up to being the one who put a hole in my head.

I had to go into a doctor's office: eight years old, fully conscious as they poured molten plastic into the top of my skull. For whatever reason, they couldn't knock me completely out. I was told to hold the doctor's jacket and when I felt the first steaming globs of hot plastic hit, I tore the fabric of his jacket.

Thanks, Farrah.

+

In high school, we went to see *Phantom of the Opera* in Toronto at Pantages Theatre. During that trip, there were students from Firelands High School who went, too.

That was my door.

That was my "in."

Girls didn't talk to me at Edison. They'd apparently already figured me out. They had preconceived notions or something. They talked to me, but they weren't interested in going out with me. I was always chasing after Mandy Koleno or Reneé Robinson or someone, but I guess I was a known quantity, just like when Welfle held me up for everyone to see: Shawn Daley, Future Fry Cook.

Going to see *Phantom* with the Firelands students was great. It was like someone pushed the Reset button. "These guys don't know who I am." It was completely refreshing and I figured I could fake *something*.

+

The first girl I dated was Jenn Whitehead. She was a Baptist minister's daughter. She lived in Birmingham, forty-five minutes away.[12] Because I liked her so much, I used to make Caskey and Lener go with me to her church.

They sat in the back of her parents' car and I was forced to sit up front. Every time her dad would say

---

[12] This seemed like a safe distance to reinvent oneself at the time.

something like: "You're going to burn in the fires," he'd look right at me.

I'd make that drive in December alone, no heat, in my piece-of-shit Jeep.

I didn't know what I was going after, but I was driving there all the same.

Later in the life, that same girl broke up with me and went out of her way to introduce me to other girls.

She just wanted to see me happy.

(More on that later.)

+

For some reason, I have a particular talent for introducing husbands and wives to one another.

I've been the Best Man in five weddings now, just from being the guy who goes: "Hey So-and-So, meet So-and-So."

Nate Jennings and Susan Kordupel are a great example. I was walking down Center Street in Milan with Susan one day, which is where Nate used to live. Less than a block from my house. It was autumn. Susan was complaining that she didn't have a Homecoming date.

I didn't do the world's most amazing romantic algebra. We're literally a few hundred yards from Nate's house and my mind goes: *You and Nate Jennings would really hit it off!*

I had no idea if they would, but what the hell. I've known Nate since forever and this girl needed a Homecoming date. That's how I think.

Of course, Nate's in his driveway with his old blue Chevelle. He'd always be working on that damn thing. But Nate was there that day and that's all that mattered.

Nate was wicked smart and a bigger dude—not fat or anything. Just a broad-shouldered kind of guy who loved flannel. Not exactly a character out of *West Side Story*, but whatever. Just as we walked up his driveway, Nate dragged himself from out under the Chevelle, wiped his oily hands off on his shirt, and shook her hand.

Next thing I know, those two kids are starting to date.

Just like that.

Maybe Susan really liked mechanics. Who knows?

They're still married.

+

Nate's Chevelle did not like women.

It was a proven fact.

Jenn and Susan were in the back seat of Nate's car and I'm up front, all dudded up for Homecoming. We'd picked Jenn up first.

The car broke down seconds afterward.

This happened over and over again that night. Five times, probably. No exaggeration. It'd break down by the side of the road and the girls would get out.

Whenever they did, the Chevelle started up and ran fine.

When the girls got back in the car, we'd make it two miles down the road and it'd die again. Nate would work on the engine and the girls would get out again. I'd try the ignition and it'd start right up.

Like magic.

It wasn't just Homecoming night, either.

Everyone from Susan to Jenn to Keri Prout, whenever a girl got into Nate Jennings's car, it'd die.

+

Jenn was one of the happiest people I've ever met. She was always cheerful and you couldn't get that girl down, not that I tried.

She hooked me up with a girl named Heather before she moved out of town.

That's just who she was.

On our first date, I showed up in my sister's Chevette. I go to open the door for her and the entire door handle comes right off in my hand.

She's standing there with this "This isn't good" look on her face—not quite horror, but close—and I'm standing there feeling like I'm about to cry.

It's freezing outside and I'm holding a door handle to an old car. Heather had to climb through my side to get in and then the car wouldn't start at all, Nate Jennings-style.

With my nerves shot, I think I flooded it and we ended up having to take her car.

I was a class act, all the way.

"BAD MOON RISING"
—Creedence Clearwater Revival

We met at Mike Prout's house around five o'clock that night. It was 1994, junior year of high school. I remember it being one of those really bleak January stretches in an Ohio winter where it refuses to snow.

Just really damn cold, nothing on the ground.

There were six of us: me, Mike, Mara Mink, Bridget Guthrie, Matt Raymond, Heather Jeska—all crammed into Mike's old Cutlass.

Our mission was to deliver winter clothes to Mike's sister, Keri, down at Ashland College. That's a two-hour round trip, there and back. Back then, we could actually justify this as a six-person job on a school night.

So, we loaded up the trunk of Mike's car with sweaters and turtlenecks and boots, then we all set out. The car was such a piece of shit that some of the fabric inside the roof was dangling down on our heads. We didn't care.

We'd all just gotten back from Toronto after seeing *Phantom* on a school field trip. We were talking about Toronto and my failed hunt to find the perfect pair of Doc Martens up there. Not one of us was thinking about how we had school in the morning.

We didn't think about things like that. Maybe that was the whole point of us driving clothes to Mike's sister: distracting ourselves from reality and keeping the party going.

Me in the passenger side, Matt in the center, Mike behind the wheel of his Cutlass. Right behind me was Heather. In the middle was Bridget, and on the other side of her was Mara.

Mara was Elaine from *Seinfeld:* dark-haired and bubbly, yet sarcastic and caustic in ways you were never quite prepared for. Heather was quiet and reserved. (At least to me she was.) Matt was one of those very strong farm kids and goofy as hell. And let's not forget Bridget, who was just about the world's biggest sweetheart, like she'd just stepped off the set of a 1950s TV show.

Three girls in back, three guys in front.

Trunk full of clothes.

Let's do this.

+

Earlier that day, some drunk driver had taken out the stop sign at the corner of Routes 61 and 601. It was a forgotten intersection with nothing other than a fleabag motel called the Gulf Inn that's really a sad excuse for a bar. Someone had come out of the Gulf Inn parking lot, wasted as shit, and swiped the sign with their car.

Of course, we don't know this. But it set the next few minutes of our lives into motion.

We shot out of town sometime around six and everything outside looked wispy and white. CCR's on the radio. Highway's dark. There's no streetlights or anything. Just our headlights catching the fog in blurs.

The intersection was black as hell because nothing was open around it. No blinking lights, no real streetlight. Just the Gulf Inn across the street.

Mara was the first to see the headlights coming at us.

+

When Mike saw the truck—one of those multi-wheeled dump trucks hauling a trailer—he immediately yanked the wheel in the opposite direction.

Fight or flight. You can't teach those instincts.

Mike hit it at just enough of an angle so that when we collided, we hit the truck's front axle. The Cutlass immediately swung around, 180 degrees, and rammed into the truck's diesel tanks which we then sent bounding down the road.

The rest of the truck ran over us.

It flattened us into the shape of an F-1 racer.

One of the truck's tires sailed through the front door of the hotel and right down its goddamned hallway. We hit that truck so hard that we launched the front tire axle into a parked Escort parked at the Gulf Inn.

The truck was headed toward Norwalk, just east of us. All of a sudden, we were headed in the same direction. The truck jammed us into a guardrail. Scarlet sparks showered us outside and … the squeal

Accidents don't happen like they happen in movies. They're worse. You have so little time to react. It's like tenths of seconds but I remember them all in fragments:

Sudden headlights.

Mara screaming: *"Oh my God! Oh my God! Oh my God!"* seconds before impact.

My head hitting the passenger side window, hard, though it didn't break.

Shattering my glass of Snapple peach iced tea with my hand.

+

I was the first to get the fuck out of that car. I knew the Cutlass would catch fire and I needed to start pulling people out.

I remember pulling Mara and Bridget out of the side window. The doors wouldn't open so we had to *Dukes of Hazzard* our way out before the car went sky-high in flames.

Mike helped Matt out.

And then, I started to freak. I couldn't get to Heather.

I remember seeing her in the back there, slumped over in the dark. I realized she was the only one in the backseat who'd been belted in. I'm reaching in through the broken window, trying to feel for a pulse. I wasn't sure I felt anything because it was so damned cold out.

Now, remember: there weren't any cell phones back then. As far as our parents all knew, we were heading to Ashland. The nightkeeper at the Gulf was the first to call 911. Everyone's crying. Heather's unresponsive and probably dead. I remember her head hanging there in the dark, limp.

I didn't know what to do.

We had no choice but to take stock of ourselves, to make sure we were okay. We were all torn to shit.

Bridget's scalp got peeled back after hitting the ceiling. Matt ate the rear-view mirror and had a concussion. He just didn't know it yet. The steering wheel collapsed on Mike's wrist. He was in shock, but he kept taking his wrist and dangling it in front of the tail lights of the car. You know that rubber pencil trick? He was doing the same thing with his wrist, just waggling it in a way that wasn't natural. We ripped off some of Mike's sister's clothes and made a makeshift sling to keep it stable.

Mara was the only one who seemed okay.

When the firemen and cops and everyone showed up, I was buggin'. At the time, I liked clove cigarettes and had just gotten some in Toronto. I remember shuffling over to one of the firemen, totally out of it, and asking for a light. Never mind that I'm completely doused in diesel fuel. The look on his face told me all I needed to know. Even if this wide-eyed guy looking at me like, *What the fuck?* would've agreed, all of my cloves were crushed.

+

I don't really understand physics but what I *do* know is that the back seat of the Cutlass sort of *V*-ed forward. When Heather's seatbelt kept her in place, the force of the impact broke her back.

They had to use the Jaws of Life on that car to get to her. They peeled the roof right off. It was a scene, man. They called in the life-flight helicopter while the rest of us were escorted into ambulances.

The two guys in the trailer we hit were put into the ICU.

I was convinced I had internal injuries. I kept thinking that any second could be my last breath.

Even without cell phones, word got out real damn quick.

It was heavy duty. I don't know who called who first, but it was like a fuse was lit. I think someone called Mike's mom and then Mike's mom called my mom and then everyone started calling one another.

By the time we got to the hospital—this is probably forty-five minutes after the first call—our parents started to roll in.

They were all in shock, just like us.

I remember Matt and I were in wheelchairs. I had a neck brace, too. We'd go behind these double doors and we'd see, through the crack in the doors, Mike's parents. To this day, I'm glad they didn't know everything that happened before they showed up. They just knew we got into a wreck.

If they'd have seen the Cutlass first—the Polaroid that would circulate among our friends and families for decades after, the one that would elicit immediate *Holy fucking hell* jaw-drops—I'm not sure what they would have expected.

We shouldn't have survived.

+

Mike saved the six of us that night. It was a split-second reaction on his part but it was all that it took.

That knee-jerk reaction—the way he turned the wheel he did—was to make sure we didn't hit that truck head-on. Again, I'm no physicist but talking to the firemen, they said one thing that has stuck with me all of these years after: *You should've exploded on impact.*

And we didn't.

The only reason why is because both vehicles hit one another so hard that we completely stalled all forms of combustion.

You could've put a flare up to our engine and it wouldn't catch fire. Our fuel pump ruptured and shit was flying every which way but loose but it didn't matter.

I think about that a lot.

We simply cancelled one another out.

+

If it hadn't been for Matt Raymond having a perfect attendance record since preschool, the entire high school would've believed the rumors that we all died in a Michael Bay Movie Fireball the night before.

With a full-blown, eyes-dilated concussion, Matt went to school Monday morning.

He refused to miss a day of class. I mean, who does that? He barely knows his fucking name all day, completely doesn't what's going on, but he's there all the same.

Of course, it was in the *Sandusky Register* and the *Norwalk Reflector*—our accident—for the next few days.

The story was that we ran a stop sign.

The only way the state of Ohio or the county is legally liable for a stop sign is that it has to be proven to be down for twenty-four hours or more. So, if there's no evidence to show that, it automatically defaults to the guy who technically didn't stop.

Mike's parents' insurance had to cover everything, including Heather, who had a fractured back. I don't think she walked for six months, and I'm pretty sure she got home schooled.

I was in a brace and pretty banged up for a week, but I really dodged a bullet. I'd been in one car wreck before, when I was ten years old right after my great-uncle Pat's funeral. I was between the seats sitting between the driver and passenger seats, not seat-belted in. Another car T-boned us. My dad put his arm up to block me from flying through the window because I wasn't seat-belted in.

I dislocated my dad's elbow.

The accident with Mike was different. It was the first time I had a thought that maybe something—or someone—was looking over us.

The following week after things calmed down, Matt was dead-set on getting his glasses back. He'd lost them that night. He's like: "They've got to be out there, dude" and I'm telling him: "We got hit by a *truck*. We're not fucking finding them."

Anyway, we went out there with Matt and, sure as hell, we found his glasses in the field.

I'm not joking. We found them next to the guardrail twenty yards away in grass, pretty much unscathed.

Heather did recover. They had to pretty much glue Bridget's scalp down. Mike was in a full blown cast for the longest time. There's some show choir videos out there of him performing with a cast on his wrist. Matt came out okay too—glasses and perfect attendance intact.

It really drew us closer after that.

Unbelievably close.

I'm pretty sure there are only a few circumstances that are that binding in life. You don't ever have to rehash the tale; you don't have to keep meeting every year at the site of the big wreck. You don't have to do anything like that. You just go through your life understanding there are close friends, there are acquaintances, and there are people out in the world who are bound to you forever.

You might not see those people all the time, and you might never see them again.

But you're bound to them all the same.

+

When we came back to school, everyone was asking questions. Tons and tons of questions. I'm not going to lie: it was exciting. And this is coming from someone who was *never* excited to go to school. We're getting showered with attention: we're all over the newspapers and girls are giving me flowers and talking to me.

Actually *talking* to me.

It almost seemed the teachers were easier on us for a while, too. It's a tiny school, so our wreck was pretty epic. Especially the fact that we didn't die. The rumor mill had been in full motion for about twenty-four hours: Mara had died; Heather was paralyzed.

The people who started those rumors were probably like: "Oh my God, they came back from the dead!"

I remember Mike's family's insurance couldn't handle all of the claims. Heather's situation was hundreds of thousands of dollars, and I know my bill wasn't cheap, either.

That was my first glimpse into real life, of being an adult. It was the reality of "Who's going to pay this bill? I'm sixteen." There were consequences. Actual consequences. My parents were bearing the brunt of something that wasn't my fault.

Maybe you're like my friend Paul and I, years later, doing cartwheels in his Jeep Wrangler on an ice-slicked Route 250 before landing into a snow bank. No one got hurt. But sometimes it goes the other way. *Most* times it goes the other way.

Coming out of moments like that, I start to think of not only how delicate life is but how everything is connected. Maybe someone or something was watching over us—I'll never know—but I remember some parents whispering "That'll teach them a lesson" or "Why were a carload of kids all driving down on a Sunday night to give Keri Prout clothes?"

I'll tell you what: if it were a sixty-year-old woman behind the steering wheel, it wouldn't have made a damn bit of difference if that truck came barreling down the road or not.

All I know is that Keri Prout didn't get her winter clothes. Either way you look at it, she had to hit Goodwill that semester.

We used to sneak out at night, running around Milan like we were in Special Ops. One night, Shawn, myself and Nate Jennings left the house when we thought Shawn's parents where asleep. We went to the cemetery to find the mythical "glowing cross" at Abbott's Tomb.

We were pretty deep into the cemetery when, suddenly, this figure jumped out from behind a large tombstone—dressed all in black. It goes without saying that we took off for the road at light speed, screaming like little girls. Not long after that we heard Shawn's sister, mom, and dad busting up laughing.

- Jon Caskey

"MOUNTAIN SONG"
—Jane's Addiction

Dad wanted me to be an engineer and told me to stay the hell away from music.

Back on the road, Dad had no money, no qualifications, no college, nothing. It was no way to raise a family, going through your weeks thinking: *Holy shit. Where's my next paycheck coming from?*

I had an opportunity through Dad's work to get an engineering scholarship with Akron University. Everyone wanted me to do that. But let's face it: I was pretty academically challenged. I wasn't David Beckman, I wasn't Mark Minneman, I wasn't Ken DeChant. I was like, "Study? Hell, I'd rather go drink beer at the block house in Huron."

Everything bored me including math, which is hilarious because I use math all the time now. I'd hate to tell Mr. Matula—my archnemesis—that I use hydraulics, geometry, biology, and chemistry every single day. I don't want to encourage him. Back then, I knew I needed to graduate to have a future but I didn't push myself like anyone else.

I figured I was a lost cause.

Whenever I brought up the military, Dad started getting a bad taste in his mouth. All of the men in his family were in WWII, except one of them—my grandfather Thomas, who couldn't go because he had a waiver for the farm. The rest of them literally sat around the table on a Sunday afternoon after Donald got a draft notice and they all joined to follow him. All the brothers went.

All of them.

Dad's namesake—my great uncle Don—was in the Army Corps of Engineers and he was part of the building of the Ledo Road, the supply chain from India to China. Ever see *The Bridge Over the River Kwai?* He did that.

The Japanese overwhelmed the infantry units and the engineers had to fight. They captured all the engineers who were building the road and executed them, one by one. They did it with honor, though. They didn't tear off any of the soldiers' medals nor did they take any of their possessions. In fact, I have my great uncle's gold watch to this day.

When they found him, they'd been executed but left alone.

The Japanese just lined them up in a row. *Bang. Bang. Bang.*

Right down the row they went.

My uncle Jack was a tail-gunner in a B-17. He made it. Somehow, he survived the while goddamned thing.

These weren't the stories that soured my dad, though. It was the one about his cousin in Vietnam. He was a tunnel rat in the 101st Airborne and 173rd Airborne. He was on the cover of *Time*. He had a flashlight up next to his head and you could see his gun sticking out.

It was a random AP picture they snapped of him, but they forgot to credit the name underneath it. Maybe they never asked. *Time* later had a contest shortly thereafter: "Can you name this GI?"

It was my dad's cousin, Gary Cebula.

+

Dad got his draft notice and he sat on it for at least two years.

They never called him.

His bags were packed and he always made sure to keep a new tube of toothpaste in there. He unpacked, repacked, and made sure stuff wasn't getting dusty or mothballed.

But they never called.

Gary would come home on leave and take Dad back around the family quarries in Vermilion, teaching him how to survive off the land.

Vietnam screwed Gary up bad.

He got divorced and was staying at my parents' place. Dad would wake up in the middle of the night with Gary putting a knife to his throat, shouting Vietnamese. He was basically sleepwalking but thought he was still in Vietnam. There he was, four in the morning, screaming at my dad with a knife.

Gary eventually died of cancer.

He'd been hit with Agent Orange.[13]

Dad watched all of that happen. And me being his only son—I was the only one to carry the name on.

To go off into the military wasn't something he was prepared to let me do.

+

I finished high school at the same level as my sister Christina ten years prior, which is to say I was in the middle of the class. I was fine with it. I knew I didn't have it in me to hammer down a full college degree. There was no way in hell. That's not who I was.

---

[13] A chemical defoliant used by the U.S. military during its program Operation Ranch Hand during the Vietnam War from 1961 to 1971. Estimates are that 400,000 people were killed because of its use and 500,000 children were born with defects as a result.

With a sister ten years older than me, I saw pretty early on that her friends were going in and washing out. I knew I'd probably just go and drink myself out of an education and into debt. Why not go someplace where you can drink yourself into war?

I wasn't going to be satisfied with just hanging out in Milan, working at the gas station. I wasn't going to prove Mr. Welfle right. There was no way in hell.

+

All my life, I wanted to be a fighter pilot. I just wanted to fly. I knew I had the discipline to do it, to assert myself, to accomplish that goal.

The only problem is that I need glasses.

Back in the day, you couldn't be a fighter pilot if you wore glasses. Now you can. Either you get Lasik or you get your prescription built into the flight helmet.

Flying is something I've always been fascinated with. My dad's cousin Tom flew the Intruders—those snub-nosed radar-jammers. Since middle school, I'd been reading books on advanced aeronautics. I loved the science, and I loved reading about weapons systems and how they were designing things like the A-10 Warthog which should by definition not fly, but does.

Seriously: if you tried to make that thing glide, it cannot fly. It physically can't. It's a fucking anchor. But they designed computer systems and a propulsion system to make that thing fly and not only have one back-up system, but *four* of them.

The Warthog's system is always correcting itself. Usually, nine times out of ten, one or two of the back-up systems actually failed. It always landed on the third or forth back-up and the pilots never knew it.

The diagnostic people did.

Most of our advanced fighters are like that. Something will fail and it doesn't give an alarm. It just automatically gets backed up.

That's called "redundancy."

There's something beautiful about that.

+

I took the ASVAB in high school, the military test, and I scored really high. Next thing I knew, I had the Army and the Navy showing up at my doorstep. The Air Force showed up and immediately wanted me to do a tertiary job for them.

Somehow, I still felt lost.

Christine Kubeck saved me, though. She was a senior when I was a junior and she had one of those hardcore "Get me the hell out of here" mentalities. She was this blonde-haired ball-buster with a sweet side. Beautiful smile.

She wanted out of Milan so bad that she shot for the Marine Corps band. That's like asking for ten dollars, being turned down, then asking for fifty-grand instead. It's extremely difficult to get into it, but she did it all the same.

Recruiters would constantly call and schedule appointments with me and my parents. Those recruiters were goddamned relentless. They'd show up in full dress uniform—medals glaring, dress hat in the crook of their arm—and it was beyond intimidating.

I'd open up the door and all I'd see was a metric shit-ton of ribbons and stripes.

They'd be very polite but the whole time they went through their spiel I'd be thinking: "Man, there's trying to sell me something." Used-car lot people.

I wouldn't dress up when the recruiters showed up. I'd wear jeans and a T-shirt. It'd be a Wednesday night, seven o'clock after dinner. The Army was coming over to tell us what they had to offer me:

"We're going to put you through this special program. We've got this stuff available that we just don't offer everyone. What's your dream? What do you want to do? If you enlist, we'll give you money. Lots of it."

It was all sugarcoated, it was all a sale, it was all a well-rehearsed charade, and it bothered the fuck out of me.

I'm a pretty decent judge of character and they came across as *sell-sell-sell* in the guise of spit-shined boots and medals and war stories.

I just wanted them to leave.

They were in my house, trying to take away my freedom. That's what it felt like, at least.

"Join us," they'd all tell me. *"Here's our package of benefits. This is what you get. This is how much your pay will be. Here's where you could be stationed."*

They used the word "could" a lot, not to mention keywords like "Hawaii," "South America," and "Italy." Come on. Italy? *"Have a cappuccino and go do your job."* I've watched enough movies about the Marines. No one's sipping coffee in Italy and having a good time in their dress uniform. That doesn't happen. You're washing dishes and cleaning shitters.

Anyway, this cycle kept happening. The whole time Christine was saying: "Hey, I know you're interested in the military. Why don't you give these guys a chance?"

That's how she talked about the Marines. She talked about the Marines as people—not an entity, or a thing, or a machine.

One night, Gunnery Sgt. Wine showed up at my house. No dress blues, no medals, no ribbons. The dude came out in a pair of grey sweatpants and a T-shirt. He was six feet tall and looked like Captain America, except he had black hair. It went straight up on the sides into a flat-top. He was built like a brick shit house—a stereotypical Marine.

And yet, there was no pressure with Wine.

He came over and we shot the shit for a while. It was basically a conversation about where he was in life, where my parents wanted to see me in life, and what I hoped to become.

In fact, we actually didn't talk about the Marine Corps the first time he came over. When he left, I was like: "Who the hell was that?"

He was refreshing.

The guy's job is hanging on me joining, but he never sold me on a thing.

+

Gunnery Sgt. Michael Brown was short, stocky and quite simply, a bulldog. When you see the Marine Corps bulldog, that's Gunny Brown.

He told me how the other services would bullshit people into joining and luring them in. He was right. Brown wouldn't do that.

Brown was the first to say: "I can't honestly tell you where you're going to be sent, man. You're going to go into the Marine Corps and they're going to put you wherever the hell they want to put you. You can get a wish list, but they'll probably send you somewhere else."

Gunny Brown was in his thirties and was working in Norwalk, Ohio's recruiting center. He was put in charge of

Norwalk, Sandusky and Tiffin—a thirty-mile radius. He ran something of a boot camp over the weekends for future Marines.

Because of Brown, I joined the Marines in 1994. Junior year of high school.

I entered what's called Delayed Entry. You join and you sign a commitment, but you can't swear in because you're not eighteen yet. You're not an official Marine, but that time counts toward the Reserves. You're supposed to serve eight years: four active and four inactive. And that year in Delayed Entry takes a year off your inactive years.

Christine gave me a ride to the recruiting station once a month. When it got closer to enlistment, we'd go more often and run, practice pull-ups, and learn what it takes to be a Marine. The idea was that we'd get an advantage so when we went to boot camp, we'd have muscle memory and expectations and, most of all, wouldn't be struggling.

We'd meet in the parking lot behind the old Apples grocery store in Norwalk. They'd hire former drill instructors to give us a taste of a day at boot camp. Looking back on it, they were about ninety-percent of the real thing. It was intense. We'd spend five hours back there in the hands of former drill instructors.

If you've seen *Full Metal Jacket* and think you know what's going to happen, you're wrong.

+

I got there at eight o'clock in the morning. The recruiters seemed like they were in an excited, all-hands-on-deck mood. It was Gunny Brown, Staff Sgt. Baker, and a couple other recruiters from other stations. Gunny Brown was the leader, the in-charge.

We were all pretty fired up (at least I was) because we got to see drill instructors in action. They were giving us the CliffsNotes on what to do when we finally got into the Marines. To be honest, the Apples rear parking lot wasn't a bad place to learn how to stand in formation. It was secluded and in the middle of nowhere.

Aside from the yelling, it wasn't much different than marching band.

+

The two key things about Marine Corps drill instructors are fear and surprise.

Even training for it, that's what it was.

It's like that Monty Python "Spanish Inquisition" skit: the recruiters are on their way out and then, all of a sudden, the recruiters would disappear. It's almost like you're always counting to ten before someone jumps out at you.

We were in the parking lot and it's one of those typically dreary Ohio days. It was chilly and it'd just gotten done raining. The pavement was wet and, without warning, the steel door slams open. I heard people yelling but I didn't flinch.

I seized up: *This is it. This is it. This is it.*

It was four of them coming out, just randomly picking people to start breaking down.

The sergeants got up in their faces, throwing their hands up. They were yelling *Don't look at me!* and, of course, we'd look right at them. I saw their veins popping out of their heads as they screamed. They weren't cussing but they're screaming like a dog about to maul someone.

It's like *Alien* where the thing's really close to Ripley's face with all that acid dribbling from its chin.

Drill instructors are just bulldogs with a huge leash, barely being held at bay, two inches from your nose. You can *feel* their breath, you can *feel* their every word.

A couple of the other recruits started crying.

There's a reason for the shock. You always remember *anything* someone tells you when you're scared. There's two ways to get people to do things, without fail: fear and pain. And the fear of pain is the greatest tool of all.

A lot of people teach dogs and animals this shit. Unfortunately, we're no different. I learned how to march that day—the way that the Marine Corps wanted you to march. Right behind the Apples grocery store.

Drill sergeants want to "hear" boots. That's key. When you come down with a heel, they want that one, precise sound of everyone hitting their heel at the same exact time. When you watch the movies and you see the troops marching and you hear those percussive sounds, one after the other, it echoes. In reality, drill sergeants don't even want that echo.

They want it so perfect, there's no echo at all.

My old boots are in the closet right now. The heels on them are all worn down to complete 45-degree angles.

+

Soon enough, I became a senior member of the Delayed Entry program. I was helping newer recruits out. It became important to me. I knew where I was headed; I knew that I had a future.

On Fridays, I'd wear my Marine T-shirt to high school. One of our history teachers, Mr. Crooks, was a former Army guy. Hardcore conservative. City councilman. Six feet tall. Maker of men.

I got a detention one day from that guy, simply for wearing my Marine Corps T-shirt and making fun of the Army banner behind his desk.

At the time, Jon Caskey and I were both going into the Marines. Caskey had pretty much been bred to be a Marine since he was five. My plan, up to that point, had been to become an Air Force pilot. For Jon, there was no Army, no Air Force, nothing. He was a Marine, plain and simple, since we were toddlers.

Caskey always had my back with Crooks. I used to give Crooks the middle finger when his back was turned, but he'd see it in the reflection of his coffee mug or something. He'd spin around and I was instantly in trouble.

His step-brother was Gunny Sgt. Brown.

+

At first, it was a relief that I'd found an actual path in life. For the first time ever, I had goals. Real ones. So it was easier for me to go out and enjoy being a high schooler, not having to worry about SATs and ACTs and shit like that.

I would deal with fear, pain, self-loathing, hatred, and regret when it came. Before that, though, I was going to enjoy every second of high school. I didn't have anything else to worry about.

It wasn't until right after Christmas when I thought, "Aw, shit."

Christine was already gone. When I heard from her—now that I look back on it—she really censored herself. I didn't know it at the time. In her letters, she talked about the Marine Corps band more than anything else.

She knew not to tell to me everything she was going through.

Everything she wrote was positive.

+

After I joined, my sister's husband at the time was our gym teacher. Good old Wes Douglas, jock extraordinaire. He coached football and all that jazz. He looked like a young Kevin Costner, whose entire life was built around coaching sports.

A large piece of me felt superior to him all of a sudden. And I'm normally not that person; I'm normally never the guy to put themselves above someone or something. Not unless I'm provoked.

I remember thinking that I was doing something that will not only challenge myself but challenge *him*.

+

Before I left for good, there were a lot of moments when Dad simply didn't talk to me. Every once in a blue moon he would, depending on the mood he was in, but it was rare that we ever spoke.

I was dating Heather Shepherd at the time and I kept thinking: *Does our relationship have an expiration date?*

Of course it did.

At prom, I felt this huge weight on me. I literally couldn't breathe. We were on a cruise ship, the *Emerald Empress*, that ferried us all around the Sandusky Bay on Lake Erie.

Everyone else was having a great time but I remember Heather and I standing on the bow of that ship. She was standing next to me, holding me close.

All I could do was sigh. I had nothing else to give.

I knew what was coming.

Well, at least I thought I did.

I didn't have the easiest home life and Shawn's house was always a refuge for me. When I was in boot camp Shawn's letters got me through. I can clearly remember feeling uplifted when I finished his letters and found the strength to carry on.

That's just the kind of guy and friend he is. Everyone who knows Shawn understands this. He wears his heart on his sleeve and will do anything for his family and friends. I'm a better person because he is my friend.

- Christine Kubeck

"FALL DOWN"
—Toad the Wet Sprocket

There are two ways to get off Parris Island: Graduate or die.

You don't get to leave. If you fail something, you simply start over again. If you break something, they fix it, and you start over again.

They call that "recycling."

Parris is a manmade island off the coast of South Carolina, near the Georgia border. Fun fact: Parris Island has the highest concentration of poisonous creatures in North America. Black widows, sea snakes, rattlesnakes, black widows, brown recluses.

When I got there, I didn't sleep for about forty-eight hours. It was nothing but paperwork. And that's what sucked. They weren't making me do push-ups, they weren't screaming at me. I'm getting my uniform, I'm getting all of the essentials. I'm not even getting my hair cut yet.

Becoming a Marine is one thing. Getting your last will and testament drawn up at eighteen is another. Who the hell thinks of that? Well, there I was, getting it done. I'm filling out the paperwork and the addresses to send to my parents to get a special power of attorney.

Hours later, I still hadn't slept.

I was sitting at a desk in a cold, stark room getting talked to about the G.I. Bill, my power of attorney in case I die, and getting handed hundreds of forms to fill out. That's how I memorized my Social Security number in those two days. I really never knew it before, but that became my service number.

So, at Hour 33, I'm in my trousers and boots and freaking out. I don't even know what planet I'm on. I'm a zombie. Then I get ushered into what they call a "holding platoon."

Even this sergeant isn't an asshole yet.

I just had this sick feeling like things were going to get worse.

+

It was a sweltering, thick-aired June when I was on Parris Island. There were some days that it got so humid that we weren't allow to train outside. There's a flag pole for weather conditions and when there's a black flag, you're not allowed to go out and run. Yet our drill instructors snuck things around the system. They still got away with training us.

If someone got in trouble on Black Flag Day, you immediately feared "The Pit." Basically, it's this giant, square sandbox. You have to go outside and do extreme calisthenics: push-ups, jumping jacks, and leg-lifts at rapid speed, as fast as drill instructors can bark orders. You're flipping and flopping around, trying to do all these calisthenics with the sun beating down on you.

The sand's sticking to you and there are fleas all through it, leaving bite marks that look like goddamned welts or bee stings.

You're doing pushups and then jumping jacks and they'll shout: "Attention!" You pop to attention and you're standing still and straight ahead, not making eye contact. You're just locked and loaded, like a stiff board, all while these fleas are crawling all over and biting the living shit out of you.

+

Advice to future Marines: don't let the drill instructors ever learn your name.

With 100-plus recruits, it's pretty easy to hide in plain sight, but once people get injured or they're too overweight and get shipped to PCP[14], it's not as easy to hide.

I learned quickly to just keep under the radar, to move just as fast as the guy in front of me and not slower than the guy behind me.

---

[14] "Physical Conditioning Platoon." (Also known as "Pork Chop Platoon.")

I was never the first dude to show up on the scene but I was never the last guy to come out.

I just stayed right with the herd, blending in with the rest of the recruits.

The sergeants pulled out the obvious fuck-ups who couldn't keep up and made examples out of them. Half the time, when the slow guy was slow, the rest of us paid for it.

+

Everything I did in my three months at boot camp was always left over right. When I tied my boots, the laces were left over right. When I sat down on a concrete floor, Indian-style, my legs were crossed left over right.

It's always left over right.

They were developing muscle memory so that when you go out on the rifle range, you don't think. Every Marine is a rifleman first. It doesn't matter what job you eventually have in the Marines, you're always trained to shoot a rifle. When you drop down into a sitting position, your left elbow goes onto your knee to shoot.

It's drilled into you: *Left over right. Left over right.* By the time they shout: "Drop!", there's no hesitation.

You don't think.

+

I was fully prepared to kill a person. I really was, and I'm not proud of it. And it's something I struggle with to this day. A lot of Marines talk about hunting animals and some of us say they actually prefer hunting people. When you're hunting an animal, you're hunting a lower intelligence of species for the purpose of sport.

When you're at war to kill another person, you're hunting someone of equal intelligence.

I never thought twice about it.

I was ready. It was part of the gig.

Just like "left over right," it was being built into my muscle memory.

Don't think. Just pull the trigger.

+

We used to get up at five a.m. Four-thirty, sometimes. I'd been deployed to Hawaii and I'd get up to run and do calisthenics before the sun came up because it'd get way too humid.

It was pretty hardcore exercise. Some days, we'd only run a mile or so; other days, we'd run three miles on the beach in boots. I'd damn near have a stroke after those runs.

My morning routine used to be that I'd wake up, have two cigarettes, and off I'd go. When we came back, I'd smoke some more, then use breakfast time to catch a quick nap.

After breakfast, I'd shower up and get into company formation, which was basically four platoons—four squares of sixteen men each, with each square in the formation an equal length apart.

Every morning, they'd come out with the guidon, which is the company flag. The company gunny would talk to us before turning the stage over to the lieutenant or commander to have their say about what's going on that day.

It usually lasted two minutes *unless* someone was getting promoted, which was always a pain in the ass.

Sometimes, literally.

If someone got promoted, we'd always be standing a half-hour at attention. If you locked your knees, you'd pass out. If you ate bad eggs that morning, you might be standing there in formation, knees wobbling, trying not to shit yourself.

Not that it ever happened to me…

+

After boot camp, whenever I called home, I always talked to Mom. Dad didn't want to talk.

I knew why.

When someone loves you enough to not want you to do something like join the Marines, they're still holding on to that reason. They don't want to see you there. They just want you home. I don't think Dad wrote me off; I think he had it in his head I was going to go off to war and he'd never see me again.

He just didn't want to put himself through the pain. Maybe he was just biding time—*our* time—until I came back.

Either way, he wasn't acknowledging that I was gone.

+

When I was in boot camp, I got a letter from Mom that made my blood run cold. One of my high school classmates, Matt Heid, had been killed in a car accident.

The guy couldn't have been nicer. We'd all turned eighteen when he died. If you made a list of all the high school classmates whom you suspected would die early, Matt would be at the bottom. He was insanely positive and I don't ever think I saw Matt sad.

Everyone—and I mean *everyone*—liked Matt.

I'm embarrassed and sad to say that I actively tried to erase any memory of Matt for a long time. It didn't work. I just didn't want to imagine that someone as kind and sweet-spirited as Matt Heid could die. The universe couldn't be that cruel, you know? But apparently it is. At any rate, I couldn't do it. I couldn't *not* think about Matt.

It's not built into my programming and I think about him a lot.

I remember getting that letter from Mom and reading about how Matt died. I remember looking at her handwriting and studying her pen strokes, telling me that one of my friends since elementary school had been killed.

I think it was a drunk driver who went left of center and hit Matt and his dad head-on. The wood splitter or the table saw in the back of the truck came flying through the front window and took him out.

His dad survived the accident.

I might have a lot of these details wrong, but what I don't have wrong is that distinct, sick sense of mortality that hit me right then and there.

When I came home for the first time, one of the first things I did was go and pay Matt a visit at the cemetery. After all, Matt and I were in little league together, on the gold team. We were the worst team in the league. The Cleveland Browns of baseball.

If we won, it was by sheer luck.

Matt didn't care. He was always the happiest kid on that team.

+

Most of the pain and misery of the Marine Corps came *after* boot camp. That's when they really get you geared up for the Infantry.

Do you know how they train dogs for dog fighting? They lock them in a basement with no windows and don't allow them to have contact with other dogs. They just lock them in there and feed them at random intervals, poking and prodding them when they feel like it.

That's what it was like to be in the Infantry.

They got us so isolated from the rest of the Corps that I didn't even feel like a Marine at times. We started coming up with nicknames for anyone who wasn't Infantry.

"Pogues" were anyone other than us. I like using it as a term of endearment now because Caskey was a pogue: he was an air-winger.

"Jarheads."

"Teufel hunden."

"Devil Dogs."

We had lots of nicknames to throw around, but I was an Infantryman. We didn't need any other names.

"THESE DAYS"
—Foo Fighters

We were on the USS *Dubuque* and had the chance to train with Navy SEALs. The *Dubuque* was an old, *Austin*-class LST[15]—one of those flat-bottomed ships that carried hovercrafts and amphibious landing vehicles.

We were all headed from Okinawa to Korea and there were SEALs on board. Those guys were hilarious. They'd set up targets at the back of the ship, aiming out the rear end, and just light them up with AK-47s, silenced MP5s, and shit.

---

[15] Landing Ship Transport

In our platoon, we had a Russian guy named Golovady. He was a real workout nut and exactly who you'd imagine when you think of a henchman from a *Die Hard* movie. He had muscles the size of my head and a thick "I will break you" accent. Golovady was part of the 1991 revolution, chucking Molotov cocktails with the best of them. No joke.

He ran into the SEALs at lunch and they invited him, Corporal Ski, and me down to take a look at their weapons that night. (Golovady clearly makes an impression.)

We loved talking guns and stuff. We went down there into what looked like an old railroad car. It was nothing but a big, steel box. The doors opened up and there's this vast array of high-tech weaponry just staring back at us, gleaming in the fluorescent lights.

The next thing I know, we're invited to shoot with them off the rear of the ship. What I didn't know was that the entire ship was also clamoring to get a chance to fire with them.

Each gunshot sounded like fingers snapping. Nothing more than the sound of a firing pin. I almost forgot I was in the Marines. I was shooting guns with good friends. I also caught on to how their commanding officer was choosing Marines to go out and get a chance to fire with them.

He'd point to a Marine and say: "What's your hometown?"

"Cleveland."

"I hate the fucking Browns! Get out of here!"

Then, he'd go to the next guy.

"What's your hometown?"

"Atlanta."

"Hey, the Falcons are good this year! Get up there!"

He chose nearly an entire company to shoot his guns based on football teams and their home city.

Around one in the morning, we're going around the peninsula somewhere off the coast, in the middle of nowhere. On the port side of the ship—where we'd usually load in groceries and supplies and shit—Golovady, Ski and I watched all of the SEALs jumping off the ship.

They wore nothing but their swim trunks, diving thirty feet above the water. Pitch black, dead of night. They had their teammates pick them up with an inflatable Zodiac boat.

One after the next.

We're hauling ass but they're just jumping out in the middle of the night into what could've been shark-infested waters. They didn't care. Off they went.

I wasn't that dumb.

+

Picture a helicopter hovering about fifteen feet above a ship on high seas. You're supposed to rappel out onto this ship but you can see the rope beneath you coiling and uncoiling as the ship heaves up and down.

You're trying to time it while they're barking at you: *"Get the hell out!"* You're sliding down with your helmet on, rifle strapped to your back, and you've got thick rubber gloves on. The idea is that you're supposed to fireman-pole your way down that rope.

The problem is that you might come down as the boat's heading upward and smack the deck harder than you thought. Then again, you could rappel down and fall another ten feet.

I've had several 200-pound-plus Marines land on my back that way. It was no fun. It was like birds shitting Marines out of the sky.

+

Ever watch a movie with a main character who's a Marine, with a theaterful of actual Marines?

Holy. Shit.

When I was on Hawaii, I watched *Independence Day*—that cheesy alien invasion flick—with two hundred Marines. You would've thought it was *Patton*. We waited an hour in line at the base theater back in 1996. A lot of the Marines were still in uniform. They'd just gotten off duty and didn't even change clothes. Will Smith played this Marine fighter pilot and I'll tell you what: that was probably the military equivalent of watching the *Rocky Horror Picture Show*.

Whenever a Marine showed up on screen, the room went bonkers. The Marine General that's in the movie comes into frame and intones: "I'm talking to the President and we're going to fucking do these aliens in."

I'm paraphrasing but, Jesus Christ, popcorn went flying through the air when he said that. It was like the movie *Gremlins*. Whenever the aliens came on screen, Marines started throwing shit. Boots, shoes, soda bottles, their covers, their hats.

Most of them were drunk.

It was insane and I loved every second of it.

Whenever anything good happened—like Will Smith outrunning an alien ship in the desert canyon—they'd yell *"Hoorah!"* and *"Semper Fi!"* Some even starting singing the goddamned National Anthem when the President gave that speech at the end.

Every time I see that movie on TV, I think about that night. It was better than a 3-D movie. When the aliens are attacking the base, just imagine things flying over your head and at the screen.

You watch it now, it looks pretty weak. It's slightly better than *Sharktopus* on SyFy. But I'll tell you what: Marines never went crazy over *Sharktopus*.

+

I was on a demolition range on Mount Fuji. We were practicing with charges. That's what our team did. We were experts in explosive devices, in designing things to take out tanks.

We always let the new guys do the wiring on the fuses. There's a certain protocol you have to follow when you're using fuses. When you get a spool of it, you cut off the first ten feet. That's because the first ten feet absorbs every ounce of moisture in transport, so it may burn slower. Then again, it may burn faster.

You never know.

The idea is that the fuse has stripes every three feet. You do a test burn because every fuse is slightly different. You need to have accuracy down to a tenth of a second on some of the bombs you're designing.

So, these new kids—they timed it, but they screwed up.

I think they cut the first five feet off the charges, not ten. One of my good friends Dustin Mathis and I were walking away when they pulled on the fuse.

The thing went off when we were maybe thirty feet away.

Forty pounds of ammonium nitrate.

These bombs are made to put a twenty-foot crater into the ground to stop tanks and personnel. The blast launched us through the air. We were hurtled by a blast that could've turned my internal organs into liquid.

When you're messing with explosives, you've got to remember that you're ninety-percent water. When a concussion wave goes through your body, it does a lot more than lift your ass into the air. It can collapse your lungs. It can do a lot of damage.

We became gunshy for a while after that. We didn't just dust ourselves off and say, "Well, *that* happened."

It scared us.

+

You're always combat-ready for deployment, but the thing is: you're not allowed to take everything you own with you. You basically take what's on your back.

By all accounts, it should've been impossible to play music, but we did it all the same when the entire battalion went from Hawaii to Japan.

We hung onto an acoustic guitar and kept writing. At one point, I think we acquired some drums and we rehearsed in a shed where they had all the big, cotton targets they used at the rifle range. It was 95 degrees in that thing, with no A/C. They had thousands of those targets—stacked like cordwood—and the smell of rotting glue was just brutal.

Chris Hill was the singer—this short, blond, surfer dude from Florida. Chris Cahill was on drums and he was this skinny, skinny, skinny drummer with bizarre reserves of energy. Josh Smith was on guitar and he was a very quiet, almost awkward dude. And Aaron Barquist was in the band, too, but it was odd because he was an E4 when I was an E3. You don't really party with your leaders in the Marines.

During the day, it'd be: "Corporal."

A nod: "Daley."

Then on the weekends, it'd be: "What's up, Aaron?"

The higher-ups somehow got us into this room in Mackey Hall with the caveat that we had to keep it spotless. It always had to be clean. Mackey Hall was like a hotel where you have the door open into a hallway. We were on the first floor and all the doors opened to the outside air.

No way in hell could we have musical instruments just sitting out in this room. If we did, they'd be confiscated. We had to get inventive.

I smuggled an old mixing board from Ohio all the way to Hawaii, then to Japan. I kept it under the bed. The wall lockers were normally for our uniforms, but that's where we stored the amplifiers and speakers for the PA. The drums we kept in a pile in the bathroom and we ran all the cables under the carpet.

We wrote a lot of music. It was punk rock with some metal. Stuff like that.

What mattered was that we passed every random inspection.

Every Friday night, we'd get off work, load up on the Mickey's Ice, and head down to the room. It was built to sleep two people, maybe three if you had bunk beds.

We had two standard beds and two wall lockers. On band nights, each wall locker had a Marine sitting on it, drinking a 40 with nothing but their damned silk shorts on. Just hanging out, completely tatted up, with at least half a dozen Marines outside the door smoking cigarettes, shooting the shit.

It was a party, every Friday and Saturday. We were playing the same shit over and over and over again. Everything from Megadeth to Green Day to Bush to our original stuff.

It was rough, but we were a band.

+

Fuji's base is tiny and we were always on the side of the mountain. We'd go out and do ops at night, just practicing navigation skills. There was no GPS back then—just compasses, maps, and nothing else. We'd basically go out and follow terrain for two or three days, then come back.

We were the Alpha Company weapons platoon and we'd just been issued these brand- new tent systems. They were dome tents with a rain fly. For the Marine Corps, they were pretty high-tech at the time. They'd sleep an entire SMAW[16] team.

---

[16] Shoulder-launched Multi-purpose Assault Weaponry

We're up on the mountainside and I'm on radio duty. I had a backpack on with a PRC-77 transceiver radio, loaded with lithium ion batteries. If they got wet, they'd launch your ass like Sean Connery in *Thunderball*—or Steve Lener, years later, in his backyard.[17]

My team's asleep and it's about 11:30 at night. The wind's picking up and it's starting to rain, spackling the fabric of our tent with these big fat drops. At this time of the year, it was in the sixties or seventies. Rainstorms weren't uncommon on Fuji then, but it wasn't on the weather report I'd been given.

I radio back to the base and ask for an update. The dude reads the newspaper report back to me in this dialtone voice, telling me that it's clear skies and no rain.

He clearly didn't turn the fucking TV on or bother to look out a window, because we were having a typhoon.

We're up on the side of Mount Fuji and a typhoon's decided to change direction and come at us.

After about an hour, it's getting worse. I can hear the trees and the roar of something bad coming our way. I grab the radio and shout: *"Mayday! Mayday!"* I was crouched

---

[17] Not really my story to tell but, yes, Steve Lener once blew himself up.

in the doorway of the tent and it's nothing but blinding rain outside.

Before I knew it, everyone's tents start to collapse. Gear was going airborne. Shit's rolling down the hill. When one group got out of their tent, the dome immediately sailed in another direction.

Big Dick was in my tent and he asks: "What's happening?"

My face looked like that old Maxwell cassette commercial, with my cheeks flapping in the wind.

We're trying to get everything together and we can't see shit. There were about thirty of us all along the ridge. One lieutenant insisted we go one way to get back to base. We all said, "No, we have to go this way."

Turns out, his way took another forty.

We're running in blinding rain and wind in the dark of night, and I still have that rocket of a radio in my backpack. There were mudslides just ripping down the mountainside and at certain points, we were waist-deep in water. We were all holding onto each other and if someone slipped, we picked them up.

Turns out, the entire base was on lockdown.

I can't get a hold of the dude inside who was giving me the weather report. He abandoned ship or some shit once he realized there was a typhoon bearing down on him. So there we were, standing outside the base with thirteen feet of razor wire fence and MPs with guns between us.

We're now trying to break *into* a United States Marine Corps facility.

The typhoon's in full swing and we throw flak jackets over the razor wire. We took these two Mexican cats—they're like 110 pounds each—and literally launched their asses over the fence.

After they made it over, I think it took them at least another hour to find somebody who had a key to the gate.

We're all out there waiting as the water's getting deeper. It's up to my knees but there's nowhere else to go. I remember the lieutenant who was *so sure* we were going the right way was pretty embarrassed by that point.

People like him are always the first guys to get shot.

"FELL ON BLACK DAYS"
—Soundgarden

The old joke with deployment was that there are three things to do: watch movies, become an alcoholic, or lift weights.

You rent VHS tapes and get obsessed with the entire *Halloween* series over a week. You go to the gym and bench-press. Or you succumb to the beast and get yourself drunk every night.

I sure as hell didn't go to the gym.

Drinking's always been an issue. Honestly, the first time I remember drinking something to *drink* something because I knew it'd *do* something was when I was ten years old. Grabbing my dad's bottle of Beam when I was five doesn't count. I didn't know what the fuck that was. It was like milk to me.

But at ten, that was when I consciously thought: "This might be fun."

It was at a block party on Edison Drive and I couldn't understand why the adults were acting so goofy. Everyone was there. The Jesbergers, the Westbrooks, us. My house had the band, the Jesbergers were in the middle and had the food, and the Westbrooks were on the end and they had a swimming pool.

My dad would put together a band and they would play in the garage and the driveway would be the dance floor. They would play everything from Grand Funk Railroad to KISS to AC/DC.

The mayor and the police chief would be there. There were no noise ordinances because the entire damn town would be at this party.

I remember the adults were plastered.

They'd take the kegs they thought were empty and put them behind the pine trees of the Westbrooks' house. And me and Adam Westbrook, who was two years older, would go back there and start finishing off the kegs.

The next time I drank was in eighth grade, when my sister got married to Wes Douglas. Dad would send Jon Caskey and I up to the bar to get all his buddies shots. We thought: "Well, since we're getting them all shots, there's nothing wrong with adding a couple more to the tray." And we'd take those out back and then bring Dad and his buddies their shots.

I was afraid of my dad finding out.

I wasn't fond of going out and picking my own branch off the apple tree.

I know they found out about the beer behind the Westbrooks'. We talked about it years later. They couldn't figure it out. They thought I'd gotten into mom's cough medicine or some shit.

For me, drinking was like something out of an Atari game: *Drink this elixir, become stupid.*

+

Before it got bad, I had a ball with drinking. Gallivanting around Waikíkí before I was twenty-one. My Friday-night tradition was getting a fifth of Southern Comfort and a one-liter of Mountain Dew. I'd pour half the Mountain Dew out and pour the SoCo in. Then I'd just walk down the strip. I didn't even have to go to the bar.

It'd be two o'clock in the morning and I'm on a beach full of people.

Later, in Japan, alcohol was a different beast. It was more evil, more insidious over there. That's where no one has any family, you're removed from everything familiar, and people are drinking simply to make life disappear.

+

I woke up in Japan on a Sunday morning. We'd been out the night before, drinking. I woke up and was pretty hungover. I was groggy, stumbling down the hallway in board shorts and a long-sleeved T-shirt. Dirty light leaked through the windows and I could barely keep my eyes open.

Those past few Sundays, we'd lounge around and watch the movie *Singles* or I'd meet up with the guys in the band.

As I was walking down the hallway, this Vietnamese guy in our platoon named Chong stopped me. (I have no idea how the hell Chong made it through boot camp, given his horribly broken English.)

In this comically thick accent, he goes: "*Dawee!* What the fuck wrong with your neck?"

I just wanted him to go away.

"Chong, leave me alone, brother."

"No. You look in mirror. *Now.*"

So, I stumble into the bathroom, flip on the light, and wince. But sure enough, Chong was right.

It looked like someone punched me on the left side of my neck and my right side was poking out. It was like an optical illusion by M.C. Escher.

I run down to my doc and he opens his door and *he's* hungover. He looks at me and instantly his eyes are as big as silver dollars.

That wasn't a good sign.

"Get out of here. Go, go, go," he told me. "I can't do anything for you."

I'm like, "But you *have* to do something. You're the doc!"

He ended up taking me over to the Army Medical Hospital and before I know it, I'm being rushed to the hospital and I have three docs standing around me.

They scheduled me for a biopsy the next morning, Monday. I didn't know what the fuck that meant but I showed up for the appointment anyway. They stuck me in a chair, stabilized my neck, and jammed a needle into the mass.

The doctor put the sample underneath a microscope right there in the room with me. He didn't say much and just scribbled a few notes, murmuring to himself. All I'm thinking about is whether I'm giving birth to my twin brother. Should I draw a face on it and give it a name?

He says it's a Non-Hodgkins situation, but definitely something we have to get rid of. I had an MRI done but I wouldn't get the data back until the end of the week.

I honestly wasn't that scared. I assumed it was an inflamed muscle or fluid building up after rough-housing or some shit like that.

I know one thing: I didn't work.

I didn't have to report to duty. I showed up for formation, "I'm here," and they'd send me back to my room. They put me on light duty until they figured out what it was, which meant I was stuck at the barracks, sitting behind a desk, logging shit in, making sure the place doesn't burn down.

I got the results a few days later.

"It's not spreading," they said about the cancer I didn't know I had, "but it's growing and it's going to cut off your jugular and carotid."

+

Basically, we had forty days to get it out of me before I didn't wake up one day, or I sneezed wrong and everything shut down.

Before that, though, the doctors wanted me to call home. They handed me a pen and paper and asked me to call home to get the history of cancer in my family.

That's when it started hitting me.

This was real.

I remember the antiseptic smell of the room and the awful clash of blue walls and brown carpeting. I remember going through all the stages of grief. Not for myself, but for everyone I knew.

I really had no intention of telling anybody at home. I had no intention of wanting them to worry about it. Before I know it, the doctors are like: *This isn't a drill, this isn't a test, do not pass Go, do not collect $100. You're fucked.*

I should have waited until the next day to do it, but I didn't. I wasn't just going to call home and go: "Hey Mom! How's it going? I have cancer!"

How do you call you parents with this kind of news and not freak them out?

Truth is: you can't.

You can't ever really prepare yourself for those moments, so I decided to rip the Band-Aid off. Part of me was thinking maybe I could hide it and not have to worry about it until I got out.

I'm a really bad liar—especially when it comes to my family.

Of course, Dad got on the phone and the next thing I know, he's trying to acquire transportation to Japan. There's no civilian flights to where I was. A parent can't just go visit their son in Okinawa. Tokyo and mainland Japan, sure. Okinawa? No way.

You have to go to the mainland, then get on a boat, then get clearance and all this other shit. Dad was actually trying to acquire a small engine plane from Japan to Okinawa, trying to go all James Bond and shit.

Turns out, we don't really have a history of cancer but that's not because anyone *didn't* have it. Mother Nature and war took most of us out before anyone set foot in a doctor's office.

+

Dad has cancer now.

He found out on Father's Day. I was out on Put-in-Bay[18] doing my deejaying gig on the island that night, when my sister called. On any given night during the summer, it's a drunken, memory-erasing, trust-fund-fueled place to be.

"Hey, Dad's yellow. He looks like a goddamn banana. I'm going to take him to the hospital."

Two weeks prior, he was complaining that he might have an ulcer. He thought it was diet-related. Even the family doctor said so. To be fair, his type of cancer is extremely hard to find and can only be detected by CAT-SCANs and biopsies.

So, they took him to the hospital. It looked like gallstones were blocking his pancreas, liver, and bile ducts. In a matter of a few hours, I got another call saying: "Yeah, they found some other shit. Dad's got cancer."

I've always had a game plan to get off the island if I needed to. Say, if my wife Erin got injured or if the house was burning down.

---

[18] Popular summer destination on Lake Erie, fifteen miles north of Sandusky on South Bass Island.

Still, even if I have to put that plan into effect, I make sure the music never stops. I kept that motherfucker moving that night. I have a playlist that goes into "auto mode." I flipped it on and I told the owner: "I'm out of here."

The one thing I didn't count on was the Jet Express[19] being completely sold-out that night. The only way back to the mainland was booked. If the Jet Express has too many people on there with tickets, they get fined fifty grand per person for being overbooked.

The Coast Guard hits them hard.

Still, I managed to squeeze onto the boat. Erin met me at the dock. She took me over to Fisher-Titus, and there's my dad. For the next week, I camped out by his side.

He looked like hell and it bothered me something fierce. It took me right back to the point of me having cancer myself—it took me right back to those first twinges of denial and grief.

I'm feeling that again but, this time, it's for him.

Here's the thing about me: when I'm going through surgery and there's needles and shots and IVs and shit, it

---

[19] Ferry service from Port Clinton to the islands

doesn't bother me. It doesn't affect me one bit. When I see other people going through it, it fucking kills me. I can't even watch it on TV. I don't know why. Maybe it's empathy.

Dad starts in with this whole, adamant "Shawn, you know what? We all have an expiration date" speech. He's pretty much resigned to dying, right from the jump.

I wasn't having it. The Marine in me kicked in and I started yelling at him. Literally yelling.

"Don't you goddamn give up! Don't you stop and think about that now," I heard myself shout. It was out-of-body. *"This could be nothing. I can beat it, so can you. Shut the fuck up and man up. Let's get past this."*

So, we had to go in phases. They had to get rid of the blockages, which they did at the Cleveland Clinic. Up to that point, my father had never been knocked out for a surgery, no anesthesia. He was terrified.

I had to go from being the son to taking the torch and trying to lead him. I felt helpless, but my training was kicking in. I wasn't a kid anymore and I had a new mission: rescue my father from himself.

+

My father can turn his emotions off at a moment's notice. In private, he's not afraid of them—especially in the past five or ten years. Growing up, I never saw him break down. In his older years, sure.

And of course, he prefaces it every time: "You know I'm not afraid to show you this, Shawn. I hope you're not afraid to show it, either."

He was doing that in the hospital too. I slept in the chair next to his bed for days at the Cleveland Clinic.

He goes back every other week. Unfortunately, my dad is a number nut, just like me. He's always like: "Doc, what're my odds?" They gave him six treatments and then a reassessment. In my dad's mind, it was six treatments and he'd be done. Six treatments were up and, lo and behold, they put him on for four more.

It took the wind right out of his sails.

I didn't have to go through chemo. They gave me the option, but they would have kicked me out of the Marine Corps. I had a year and a half left. I went into the Marine

Corps and immediately waived my right to get money for college.

I wanted to do it for the right reasons.

Looking back on it now, I think: *Son of a bitch. I could have used a VA loan for a new house or something.*

I like doing things purely, not because there's a secondary reason.

+

Dad would be drinking a cold beverage but to him, it'd be like drinking scalding hot coffee. He'd put his hand in the freezer and it'd feel like a thousand rubber bands being snapped against his skin.

That was just the beginning.

Now, when he gets cold, he loses all feeling in his hands and his feet. Honestly, it got my dad to eat better. He dropped down to 185 pounds and not because he lost his appetite due to chemo.

There's a cocktail for chemo these days that's anti-nausea and won't affect your appetite. He chose a better life of eating healthier because the cancer scared the shit out of him so bad.

In those first days between biopsies, we talked about life and we talked about death. When he was sleeping, I thought about what life would be like without Dad and what life would be like *with* Dad after he beat cancer.

I know this sounds bad, but I remember thinking cancer could be the best thing that's ever happened to him.

It was a wake-up call. For everyone.

+

Let's go back to me having cancer in Japan. I *beat* it, yes. I'm talking to you now. You know the end of that story because you're reading these words, but it wasn't easy.

At all.

The same week I found out I had cancer and they set a date for me to get my surgery done, I decided to get drunk again. Hard. When I'd get turned away from the enlisted men's club, I'd just go and grab a bunch of Olde English 800.

A week prior to finding out I had cancer, my girlfriend of three years left me. All my shit was still at her apartment. I found out she was cheating on me with one of my good friends from Hawaii.

The first thing I felt was anger, but not anger at her. I was pissed at myself for letting it happen. What did I do wrong? Was it something I said or did?

That was followed with: *I want to tear the person she was cheating on me with apart.* Sadly, this has happened a number of times to me. I've broken it off with one girlfriend in my entire life. The rest of the time, if I find out my woman was with someone else or they were flirting with that idea, I'd always hear about it through a third party.

Anyway, I decided to call this girl to tell her what was going on.

She was a psychology major and finishing up her doctorate. She literally told me on the phone: "That's a great lie, Shawn. That's a great way to try and make me feel bad and put me in your position. I don't believe for one second you have cancer. And I think you need to go to hell."

That's pretty much verbatim.

And then she hung up the phone on me.

A week after that, I lost my dog Amber.

My life was a country song for a solid month.

+

Dad sat next to his mom when she died. He watched the whole thing go down.

So when we were in the hospital, he kept saying to me: "I don't want you to go through that, Shawn."

"We're not, Dad."

I'm the type of guy who doesn't have time to hear that shit. I'll just walk out of the room or tell you to shut the hell up.

We're not there yet.

Philosophizing about your untimely death is not worth it. You might as well pull the plug now.

No one knows how they're going to go.

"EVERY DAY IS EXACTLY THE SAME"
—Nine Inch Nails

When you get ready to leave the Marine Corps, you have to go through these weeklong classes of how to become "normal" again, how to become a civilian, and how to look for a job.

It was surreal.

After cancer, the Infantry didn't want me anymore. The Marines wanted me to be the bass player for the Corps Band and there was the possibility of a $30,000 signing bonus being thrown around. Still, I was damaged goods in their eyes and I couldn't re-enlist.

If I'd have stayed in, I would've been fat and happy playing bass—right up until 9/11. Then I would've been thrown back into the Infantry and hurtled over to Afghanistan. I also probably would've gotten hurt because I'd be all fat, nasty, laid-back, and playing bass.

That last week, the Marines flew me to California, where I spent another week going through what they call "check-out." It's just like joining, all that insane paperwork, but now it's in reverse. They got you in, now they're getting you out.

It was a Friday and there was still some bite in the air the morning I walked into Camp Pendleton, California.

The entire time I was in the Marines, I was an E3. They'd even shut my job down and phased it out. Basically, I'd never gotten enough points to be promoted the whole time I was in. I'm getting out of the Marine Corps with an Honorable Discharge, an achievement medal, and a stack of Good Conduct ribbons.

I'm standing in front of this guy, this E4 corporal, expecting him to read my discharge from active duty and instead, he reads me my promotion award.

I got promoted, right on the spot, to Corporal.

He took off one of his chevrons, put his own Corporal chevron on me, then I got discharged from the Marine Corps a minute later.

I was in tears.

When I got home and received my discharge certificate, it said "Corporal Daley."

I don't know how it happened, but it did.

+

I returned home and had no idea what the hell I was going to do. I remember landing at Cleveland Hopkins Airport and my niece Ally was bawling her eyes out. Someone had spilled hot coffee on her in the security line—not because she was overcome by the sight of me.

My parents had gotten a divorce while I was gone, too. Thirty-five years of marriage, over. Just like that.

Dad still wasn't talking to me too much.

I had no money. I mean, *none*. I had to become a civilian again and my family gave me a week to get my shit together. I felt like I'd just graduated high school all over again, getting out of the Corps.

My resume had two bullet points:

Edison High School.

United States Marine Corps.

I used my mutual funds to buy an '86 Monte Carlo that died within the first year I owned it. I was broke and sleeping on Mom's couch. When you go from waking up every morning and doing menial things for the defense of your country, this highly scripted series of events, to not having any script at all, it's unsettling.

I had someone telling me how to tie my shoes, what to wear, and where to go for four straight years and then, all of the sudden, I didn't have that anymore.

I still iron my shirts, every morning, simply out of routine.

+

Dad had started a water treatment company called Uni-Tech Environmental Services back in the Nineties. The idea was to get some extra Christmas money, I guess. They weren't too big yet—it was just my sister Christina and Dad.

Dad offered me a hundred bucks a week to join the family business and I took it.

My first year, I cleaned filters at the wastewater treatment plant. Then, one of our clients that we did reporting for the EPA lost their superintendent. So, I became the youngest superintendent in the entire United States. I went from that hundred bucks a week to making a pretty decent paycheck in maintaining all the drinking water for a small town.

I felt like I had a purpose again.

I ran the water treatment plant for five years. It was built in 1947 and it was like running the fucking *Monitor* or *Merrimack* as far as technology went. It was all hand-cranked. I was the janitor, the chemist, the secretary, the superintendent, and the groundskeeper.

The plant would eventually close down and rough times were, again, right around the corner.

I really don't remember what I was thinking when I first saw him. I just knew that I had to meet him. It wasn't long after that night that I knew I loved him. In fact, it was only about two weeks.

I was the one to say "I love you" first. I just knew. I was afraid I would scare him off but fortunately for me, he didn't run. If Shawn were gone tomorrow (and I'm tearing up at the thought) I'd miss his compassion. He always cares and knows exactly what to say to motivate and get me—and everyone—through any situation.

Oh—and his hugs. He gives great hugs. He is the love of my life. I don't know what I would do without him.

- Erin Lykins Daley

"BE MY YOKO ONO"
—Barenaked Ladies

I was in a cover band called Short Bus with Paul Fuhr and Steve Lener for a minute. We fumbled our way through a lot of R.E.M. and Oasis songs and The Verve's "Lucky Man" and Filter's "Take a Picture." We caught a lot of flak for the name "Short Bus."[20] I remember getting heckled by two nurses at a gig who didn't think it was necessary (or funny) to make light of special-needs people.

Until I told them our name, they were totally into us.

---

[20] Steve's idea for a band name. Not ours.

We were playing the Old Dutch, this shit-hole bar in Sandusky, and we're the only band to have ever played it. A decade later, that's still the case. Paul had an "in" there through a bartender named Charlie, this totally gregarious dude who also worked at his parents' place. That night, there was this girl there, Erin, with her sister. Apparently, I'd caught Erin's eye during a cover of The Who's "The Seeker" or something.

We got done with the gig and it wasn't that late so Erin invited us all to go to Bucko's. Bucko's was an even stranger dive than the Old Dutch. It was someone's fucking house where the living room was the stage. It was weird. A band called Monkey Love was playing.[21]

Well, Erin was engaged at the time, but I didn't know this fact.

She cornered me by the stairs, out of view of the band and the tiny-ass dance floor and she kissed me. It was a *Scott Pilgrim vs. the World* moment. I look right over her shoulder and there's Baby Huey—her fiancé—slam-dancing to "867-5309."

---

[21] I'd later be a member of this band.

He and one of his buddies were head-butting each other like a bunch of Neanderthals. I looked at Erin, back at him, then back at her and thought: *Ah, fuck it. What have I got to lose?*

Well, this dude could easily pick me up over his head and rip me in half. He was like Bane. I wasn't thinking all that straight—I felt woozy with Erin—because he was probably a solid foot and a half taller than me.

We closed down Bucko's that night and ended up at her sister's house. It was a great after-party. Erin and I talked the whole time. We talked about our parents, our families, our favorite movies, how much we'd hated high school, what our dreams were.

Everything.

Her fiancé had vanished—or hadn't been invited. I couldn't tell which.

We were in the kitchen near the front of the house, where there's this big picture window. It was dark and I felt awkward. I suddenly felt like I should leave. It's like a sixth-sense sort of thing.

Before I know it, as if right on cue, there's a commotion outside. Erin took off like a shot and I heard her yelling.

She's holding off the fiancé by the front door.

This dude thought *Steve* was making a play for Erin. He's there, drunk off his ass, waving a Louisville slugger. He'd shown up to beat the hell out of Steve Lener and his giant head.

He had no idea.

I'm ashamed to admit this, but when the cops hauled this guy away for "drunk and disorderly," my first thought was: *Well, looks like I'm in there now.*

Erin's mine.

"BREATH AND A SCREAM"
—Pearl Jam

I'd just gotten off Middle Bass Island in mid-summer. It was one of those great days on the Lake—sparkling emerald water, not too humid, calm and even breeze.

We'd just landed a client over there. Me, my dad and sister had been over there negotiating. It was our initial meeting with the guy and we'd gotten contracts signed. It went great.

So we jumped off the ferry and strolled up to the Catawba Inn. It's this little bar just up the street from the ferry docks and we were having a celebratory lunch.

I was having a big old steak and we were toasting.

Then, out of the blue, I got a text from Keri Prout.

We lost Mikey last night.

It was one of those rare moments where you sit there and the entire world drowns out around you. It's that Tim Burton effect where you're sitting in a chair and everything around you telescopes away.

Everything just went dark.

In an instant, I'd been gutted.

My dad and sister literally were sitting right next to me but they could have been a hundred miles away. They could've been on the moon. Everything in that bar just went flying out of view.

I was three shades of white.

My sister says: "What's wrong?"

I didn't say anything.

I was just sitting there shaking, seeing the phone. I hear "What's wrong?" again and I suddenly smacked the table. I heard the silverware scatter and excused myself.

I ran outside and got on the phone and called Keri. Turns out, I was one of the first ones she messaged.

It was true: Mike Prout, one of my oldest friends, was dead.

Immediately, I was overwhelmed with waves of despair and disbelief. Those feelings were replaced with a need to spread the word to everyone. I felt this strangely electric, kinetic impulse to be there for everyone else, to call everyone and let them know what had happened.

Mike had made a life for himself. A good one.

He was living in the Virgin Islands, on St. John, as a chef. He'd opened a restaurant with two of his friends called La Plancha and they were winning awards. Like everything Mike put his mind to, he was coming out ahead. He had a four-year-old son Parker and a beautiful, patient wife named Megan, who was due with their second child.

Mike had taken a bad fall down the stairs at his house. One of Mike's business partners found him the next morning.

+

The last week I saw Mike Prout was the week of his wedding. He was ecstatic. I saw some footage of it not too long ago on YouTube. I deejayed the wedding, which they held at Edison Park.

The Edison BBQ Grill Team catered the damn thing. This team was a Mike Prout Production, 100% of the way. We used to go down to watch Mike play tennis at the park—Caskey, Tom Schenk, Adam Metzger, thick-bearded Scott O'Brien.

We couldn't skateboard down there nor could we be idiots and fuck around on the swings, so we started buying red meat and some charcoal and challenged Edison's rivals to bring some of their people down and cook against us.

It goes without saying that the BBQ Team didn't last long.

Word got around that we were grilling and, for some reason, Police Chief Ward decided to ban us from showing up. Ward was this barrel-chested dude with a thick black mustache who really couldn't figure out how to be anything other than an authority figure.

There was no in between with that guy.

We were apparently up to no good, grilling meat.

It was like *Footloose*. No barbecue in Milan.

+

My last memory of Mike was talking to him on the phone.

Just talking.

He was actually planning on visiting Milan again. I was helping him design his water treatment for La Plancha. He was talking about different ways to treat cistern water with UV light instead of chlorine, because it was healthier. I was helping him get a hold of the different parts for that.

I can't describe how it feels to have someone from your past ask professional questions. Questions I had answers to. It felt great to help Mike out, and I wish I had the money to have helped him out further.

Right around that time, chef Mario Batali[22] had been at Mike's restaurant and was Tweeting about La Plancha and taking pictures with him. Things were looking up for my brother.

---

[22] Renowned Italian chef who owns restaurants across the world and has appeared on TV shows such as *Molto Mario* and *Iron Chef America*.

Mike was extremely smart, but easily bored. He had his dark moments real early in life and eventually found his way into the culinary world. He found his groove, his niche.

I was proud of him.

When he passed, it was like the sinkhole to end all sinkholes. *Everyone* came back to Milan. It was like the fucking space-time continuum tore itself open. I saw friends I hadn't seen in over a decade. Melanie Lowey flew in from Washington; Nikki Lloyd came in from Colorado; Christine Kubeck drove from Pennsylvania.

Mike is the closest person I've ever lost.

I helped him learn how to drive. (Then again, I think Mike totaled five cars, so I'm not sure how much help I was.)

We had a bonfire out at Tiffany Gray's house, out there on Milliman Road, in Mike's honor. Tiffany is one of the sweetest people and it couldn't have been more perfect having the bonfire out there. She's always been this tall, slender, dark-haired girl with an insanely comforting way of speaking to others.

I loved the idea of the bonfire because it wasn't completely morose. We were laughing with sudden moments of "Holy shit, is this really happening?" interspersed within the night.

We were cracking jokes and hauling out the scrapbooks. Half the time, Mara and Michelle Schultz and the other girls didn't want to look at the pictures of themselves. They'd be like: "Oh, I don't want to see that. Put that away. I just woke up in that photo."

We'd be laughing at something hysterically, then we'd catch ourselves thinking: "Wait, what are we here for again?"

I knew Mike's music better than anybody, too, apparently. To me, that's mind-blowing. He's got two sisters, a mom, a dad, a wife, and a huge network of family and friends he grew up with and everyone's telling me that *I* know his music better than anyone.

So, I programmed Mike's showing.

No shit. I programmed Mike's showing with Richard Cheese's lounge-act versions of Weezer and Metallica. Basically, that's an hour of someone like Bill Murray's old lounge act from *Saturday Night Live* singing "Head Like a Hole."

I played Tool, I played Nine Inch Nails. I did all the songs he loved growing up. I loaded three CDs full of music that meant something to the two of us and handed it over to the funeral home.

That was hard to put together.

I also remember downing an entire bottle of Tullamore Irish Whiskey at that bonfire. I kept that bottle and put it in my Christmas tree as an ornament.[23]

The point is this: losing anyone in life is sad, but losing someone as close as Mike reminded me about a lot of things. Family, for one. To me, friends *are* my family. Even when we're not checking Facebook posts or swapping text messages, I know my loved ones are "out there" in the world. That gives me peace.

Everyone I've known is somewhere doing things I can't see. They're living their lives, spending time with their families, maybe having a few beers. I don't know. But just thinking about them or wondering what they're doing *right*

---

[23] My wife didn't know it was there when she went underneath the Christmas tree for some reason or another, and the damn bottle knocked her on the head.

now is comforting. It gives me some balance to know that life is going on beyond me.

With Mike, knowing that he's no longer out there—it fucks with me hard.

Losing friends is like losing parts of yourself you always took for granted.

I know I'm never going to experience something like learning about Mike twice in life. I'll never feel that same throbbing band of raw nerves, ugly and exposed to the world. It's impossible. I'm sure I'll feel similar emotions down the road, but not that one. These sorts of feelings come from somewhere too deep. They're too goddamned rare.

I'm convinced you only have so much to give in this world. You only have so much so much love to share. Only so much patience to give. Shit like that. That's why what we share in life is so important. That's why it means something.

Mike's death tapped into somewhere that everyone pretends doesn't exist. It's a place that makes us feel vulnerable. It's a place that reminds us of our mortality.

His death drew something out of me that I'll never get back.

It's like when you go to a concert and you come away with a ringing in your ears. Do you know what that is? That's the sound of dead cells in your ears trying to send information to your brain. It's literally the sound of a frequency you'll never hear again. Think about that. It's the sound of no sound. It's the ghostly reminder that you've just lost something that had been there all along.

And now it's gone, forever.

My brother Shawn never ceases to amaze me. There are days where he is beyond intelligent and then there are days I think he fell off the turnip truck. He has so much energy that I worry he might need sedatives. His creativity is never-ending.

Whenever he gets into a jam or if things are at his worst, he comes out of it smelling like a rose.

I'm also the biggest enemy of the mohawk. I'll be honest. I always want him to cut that thing off but, hey, if it gets him to where he needs to go in life, who am I to judge?

I still want a thank-you from him after cleaning out all the empty cigarette packs that he'd hidden behind his desk after he left for the Marines. At least 200 empty packs were shoved back there, but he was adamant: "No, Mom and Dad—I don't smoke."

- Christina Daley

"LIFE DURING WARTIME"
—Talking Heads

My dad called me on a Sunday night, just before my thirtieth birthday.

"You sitting down?" he asked. Then: "I found your sister."

I swear to God, my first thought was: "Okay. Did she forget her Garmin? Was she lost all day or something?"

"No," he said. "I found your *other* sister."

The problem with me is that when I go through emotional situations, like with the cancer and shit, I tend to shoot toward acceptance at warp speed. Normal people go through phases. Some people spend an entire week in grief or denial or bargaining.

Me? I just want to get to the end of it.

I literally push myself through denial, hate, anger, sadness, and regret in an extremely short amount of time. It was literally: "What the fuck, Dad? This is *awesome*."

He gave her my e-mail address and he gave me hers. At the time, I had MSN Messenger on my laptop. I typed in her e-mail and, boom, she's available. She's online. She's right there. She's a keystroke away from me.

Do you know what that feels like?

Her name is Sarena.

I sat with Erin on the couch with that laptop for almost a half-hour. I kept thinking: *Oh my God, oh my God.* I kept hovering over the message button, but I didn't know what to say.

She could be a crack addict. She could be a billionaire's wife out in the Cayman Islands or something.[24]

---

[24] The latter would be amazing.

Back in the Sixties, it was apparently my grandmother's decision to give Sarena up for adoption. My parents weren't married so she ushered Mom to Our Lady of the Wayside or some shit outside Cleveland—whatever nunnery it was—to give birth.

That's what you get with Catholic parents back in the day, I guess. I'm sure it made some sort of dark sense at the time. Dad was on the road playing music and he was earning the keep for the family out playing shows. My mom was back and forth from D.C. at the time.

I can't imagine what went through their head at the time. It must have been horrific. You're not married and you're being told what to do. Back then, it's probably built into you that this is what they had to do.

This is the right thing. You aren't shaming our family.

To this day, my great aunt and grandmother won't talk about it.

At one point in time, I got really angry at them. I mean, who the hell are they to plot out someone's future?

I understand if you can't afford having a kid, or aren't in the physical or mental place to have a kid, but Mom could have. Dad could've come back from the road. If you have a fucking will, there's always a way.

Sarena was given up for adoption to a family that lived in Wellington.

Here's where shit gets crazy.

Soon afterward, my parents and her adoptive parents settled down in the same town. They didn't know it. I had cousins that lived in Wellington. Apparently, there was a wedding and her family and ours were there at the same time.

When Sarena was about four or five, she played on the same playground as my sister. They both went to school together. Two years apart, but they were there at the same time nonetheless, unaware.

Her family eventually moved to Lakeland, Florida. She married a guy from Sweden. They met online. He had three kids and Sarena had a son from her first marriage as well as an adopted son, Ethan.

She grew up knowing she was adopted.

Christina and I had no fucking clue whatsoever.

Anyway, Dad had hired a private investigator to hunt her down. Her actual birth name was Denise. They narrowed it down when my mom was at the hospital. It came down to August 4, I think.

This is going to sound bad, but there were two girls named Denise born that day: a white girl and a black girl.

Obviously, we knew which one was whose.

Sarena was the name her adopted parents gave her.

Anyway, I'm sitting there with Erin and the computer and the green "Available" button in front of Sarena's name, just taunting me. Then, out of nowhere, a message pops up:

HI SHAWN.

I had a fucking meltdown.

I sat there on the couch having almost a panic attack. Erin was laughing at me, saying: "It's no big deal. Just talk to her!"

I didn't have a huge family growing up. All of my great uncles were dead, except for one. My grandparents are all dead. My cousins are so distant that I see them once a year at a horse show or a fair or some shit.

To know that there's another one of us floating out there? That's like winning the lottery to me.

+

"Why did you hide this from me for so long?"

That was the main question to my parents.

The technology wasn't there to find her, I guess. That was the excuse. And honestly, I would have gone nuts knowing that there was another Daley out there, breathing the same air as me. I don't know how my parents did that for forty-some some years.

When Sarena re-emerged, Mom kept breaking down. It was hard enough knowing she was out there somewhere, but now Christina and I had that same burden put on us.

For Dad, however, I know Sarena was one of the biggest demons constantly eating away at him.

Finding her was a huge closure.

+

Now what?

We did what Daleys always do: we took action. We got our asses on a plane and flew down to Florida. Dad went first.

Once again, I think he kept a lot of it under his hat, emotionally. Sarena didn't harbor any resentments, even though he's expecting to go down to Florida and get his ass kicked for abandoning his daughter.

Amazingly, she understood. She was just so happy to meet her real parents. Everything else was behind her.

It took guts for Dad to have called her. That's a very brave thing to do. Imagine sitting around all those years wondering what she's doing and then the enormity of all of those years, all of them accumulated, stacked up against you.

She's a woman now. She's built and lived a life you weren't aware of, that you weren't part of.

Me, Christina, Mom, and my nieces Hannah and Ally all flew down there together. Just getting down there was a chore because Christina doesn't fly. She'd never flown in her life and we had to give her many shots of alcohol to pour her on that plane.

In Lakeland[25], right in Sarena's front yard, my mother embraced her daughter for the first time in forty years.

---

[25] Fun fact: Lakeland is the Lightning Capital of the World. It's positioned right smack-dab in the middle of where large air masses cross, allowing for more direct lightning strikes than anywhere else on the planet.

Sarena and her husband were standing on their front porch with her sons were standing right next to them. It was like that "American Gothic" painting and it was a beautiful, sunny Florida day. There were storms lurking nearby and you could hear thunder off in the distance.

That was a solid five-minute hug between Mom and Sarena while the rest of us stood around, taking it all in. Everyone just stayed back and then I had my turn, and then Christina. Think about that: I'm the baby brother now, and Christina's the middle child.

I then realize: "Oh, shit. I have two nephews now!" One of them looks identical to me at ten years old: buck teeth and a bowl-cut hair.

I can't imagine someone like me wandering the planet other than me.

To think that there's a quarter-sized version of me running around in the backyard, skateboarding, building ramps. He's fucking phenomenal in music, too. He goes to the Florida equivalent of the *Fame* school. He sings opera and he's learning Latin to do it.

He's a Daley.

+

Watching Sarena with her family, watching how my sisters interacted, and even how they dressed was absolutely surreal. How things were arranged in the house, where things were kept, was exactly how we did it.

The habits. The idiosyncrasies. The tiny, imperceptible things you catch. Shared phrases. Sarena's afraid of thunderstorms like Chris is. Both of them hate flying and neither of them will do roller coasters.

We took family photos down there in a Wal-Mart parking lot and both Sarena and Chris showed up wearing identically colored shirts with the same collar.

They were fucking twins.

I hear a lot of my aunt Pat in her voice. There's also this Daley trait of a "lazy eye," where our left eye droops a little when we're tired. It's carried down genetically. My nieces have it, I have it, my dad has it, Christina has it.

Turns out, Sarena has it, too.

I've gotten to meet her twice. That's it. I'm not too thrilled about that. I want my company to grow to the point where we can just fly her in.

Until then, I miss her.

It's pretty amazing how a person cannot exist to you mere seconds before but, once they do, you love them more than you ever thought possible.

"Who would have thunk that the two-foot mohawk, low-slung bass guitar, and log chains for jewelry were all just a thin disguise for the nicest dude in the world? Seriously. He's like my favorite pair of shoes from the Nineties: tough-looking and a little leathery but really, really dependable and comfortable and I miss them when I haven't seen them for a while."

- Dustin Baker

"UPRISING"
—Muse

The Fuse Network was hosting a national Battle of the Bands. It was the first year they ever held one and, importantly for us, they had online voting. That was key for us.

    I'd joined this band called Poormercy and we'd made it past the online phase, which was as encouraging as it was amazing.

People were supporting us. They were digging the music.

Around the same time, we'd met Brian Susko, this L.A. casual/Jim Morrison kind of dude, who was recording and producing two tracks for us. While everyone was hanging out in the lounge, I was in the studio asking Brian: "What did you do there? Why didn't you do that? What if we tried this?"

I like to think I can pick music apart on a subatomic level.

It was nonstop. For two weeks, I learned so much from Brian. I studied his every move, observed his every impulse. We'd submitted those two tracks to the contest and the next thing I know, Jim Parker, Allan Carder, Sean Steffanni, and myself were in it to win it.

We were the perfect package. We knew the business side and the entertainment side equally well.

It was one win after another after that.

+

We were in Detroit at St. Andrew's Hall, where they filmed *8 Mile*. That movie had just come out and we're in the local Battle of the Bands there. And we win it.

We took the whole damn thing.

We go onto the second round, which brings another ten bands in. These are the semi-finals. When we got that initial win under our belts, it electrified us. St. Andrew's is beautiful, two-thousand seat venue. All art-deco.

They're playing our song "Ides" on 89X now—the very same station I heard Soundgarden, Alice in Chains, Nirvana and Pearl Jam for the first time.

The future could only get brighter, I thought.

+

We hired a *feng shui* expert for the studio. We wanted to keep the positive energy flowing. She was this small, black-haired Chinese lady, like a character out of *Big Trouble in Little China,* and she tailored all of her designs based on our Zodiac signs and birthdates. She even suggested for the next show that every one of us wear red underwear.

Except for me.

She singled me out and says, very seriously: "He needs to wear blue underwear."

Everyone starts laughing, puzzled.

"He needs to wear blue," she says. "He's already a fire sign. If we wears red underwear, he's going to rip everybody apart."

Apparently, I'm a fire sign and my Zodiac sign is a dragon. I needed to counteract that with water.

I thought, *What the hell.*

I did it.

Our guitarist Jim—he has one of those scientific minds—didn't buy into any of that nonsense. The second after our next win, though, he turned to me and said: "I'm wearing red underwear every day of my life."

We headed into the finals.

+

The finals were surreal. We booked four buses—these giant, real-deal tour buses full of our fans to go up there. We paid for it out of pocket. All anyone had to do was buy a ten-dollar ticket to the show and that was it.

We shipped two-hundred and eighty-eight of our fans to Detroit with free beer.

It wasn't cheap.

We got there the night before. Ahead of the finals, the Fuse Network was examining each band—all ten bands—for a possible reality show built around them, should they win the contest. They needed videos, they needed photographs, they needed interviews. We got paired up with a film crew and a photographer and went out and about Detroit as if we'd already won.

It was so weird.

They videotaped us walking down dark alleyways, emerging from manhole-cover steam clouds like we were in an episode of *NCIS*. Here we were, stomachs churning about the next night's performance, but we're touring Detroit with a film crew in tow, having to act as if we'd already won a million-dollar contract.

+

We got to the State Theater, everyone was getting in their seats, and we're all beyond nervous.

At the same time, the World Series was going on in Detroit.

The streets were dead. The stadium was lit up like a fucking moonbase or something. You could see it from miles away, but you couldn't hear anything. It was so weird. I remember it being cold and dead everywhere with this glowing beacon in the distance.

Me and Allan were having a cigarette outside when our tour buses started pulling up. The doors flew open and people started running over and we start signing things. We're signing arms, chests, concert programs.

I couldn't wrap my brain around what was going on. I was shaking hands; I was giving hugs. It was a blur. My parents were there and so was my sister. Nearly every one of my friends was there, too.

It was epic.

I hadn't even hit the stage yet.

+

We took the stage sometime well after ten o'clock. The drummer in the band before us broke his sticks and he jammed them through the drumheads before he left. The skins were completely destroyed.

It's a competition, so I remember thinking that was the drummer's way of going: "Sweep the leg, Johnny."

I'm getting set up, hundreds of people cheering in the dark, and I look over to see those drumsticks jutting out. The venue provided all of the equipment. Nothing got changed, nothing got replaced.

We made do.

We had everything choreographed, so we just went out there and did it.

Turns out, we had the most people out there then any of the other bands. Those front rows were a den of Poormercy fans.

So, we start playing under those lights and I'm not holding anything back. This is what I've been wanting my entire life. I'm doing what I've always imagined myself doing. I'm running around the stage, animated, using all of the space.

That wasn't the smartest thing.

Suddenly, I break one of the straps on my bass.

The strap yanked the screw clean out of my bass and it flew backward, over my shoulder. All the weight's now in my hands. Everything around me goes into slow motion. I dropped to my knees, leaned back with the bass on my chest, and tried to finish out the song.

I remember leaning back on the stage, sweat burning my eyes, and seeing these twenty-foot HDTV screens above us. The screens on every side of the stage. They had the camera trained on me when I fell, so I now see myself on my knees, veins popping out of my neck, and my head almost touching the stage on these towering screens.

It's hard to describe what it's like to see yourself exploded twenty times on a TV.

I finish the song out and get off my knees.

I'm dying, but I had a back-up bass. I made sure it was tuned for the next song and I was more resolved than ever.

I'm throwing myself around the stage again and three-quarters of the way through the song, during the last chorus, *POP!* I yanked the screw out of that bass, too.

Same goddamned thing.

I instinctively drop again. The crowd goes nuts, thinking I'm trying to be Flea from the Chili Peppers or something. Everyone thinks I'm trying to be a rock star when I'm really just trying to hold up a forty-pound instrument.

+

We didn't win.

    That's it. That's all I have to say. We didn't win.

    But it didn't destroy me.

    Far from it.

"LATERALUS"
—Tool

What came first: the deejaying or the mohawk?

Erin and I were struggling with money. She'd lost her job and mine was barely paying anything. They were dark days. We were sitting around one night and I suggested that I should go out and start deejaying on weekends for extra cash.

She loved the idea, jokingly saying that I should get a mohawk and a funny name like "DJ Spock" or something. I laughed and said I'd keep my name but I'd take her up on the mohawk dare.

Anything to keep a roof over our heads.

+

I had nothing left to lose, really. I mean, we literally had nothing so I thought: *Screw it*. I went to my hair shop in South Amherst, plopped down into the old leather chair, and stared at myself in the mirror as the girl wandered over with the clippers.

"Usual?" she asked.

I took in a sharp breath, then said: "No."

She crinkled her face for a second.

"No?"

"No."

My breath was even and my thoughts were clear. Then I uttered the word: "Mohawk."

"I'm sorry?"

It was as though I'd told her my chest was strapped with a vest of C-4 and my thumb was on a detonator.

"I want a mohawk."

"Well," she said, "it's gonna cost the same either way: fourteen dollars."

As if that would deter me.

I shrugged as if I didn't care and watched as she began trimming. She started low over my left ear, carefully looking at my hairline and then me in the mirror, then back again. I could tell she was nervous. In fact, she was probably more nervous than me. She couldn't tell if I was having some sort of Britney Spears meltdown or if I was serious or if this was some sort of prank her co-workers were playing on her.

"We're still low enough that we don't have to do this," she assured me after the first few tentative cuts. "We can always make it into a fade."

"Nope," I said, resolutely. "Keep going."

I fought the sickening knot curling inside my stomach, but I knew it was the right thing to do. This was more than a dare from my wife—this was a challenge pushing me somewhere I'd never been.

With each swipe of that electric clipper, she became more precise and more deliberate. She was cutting deeper—I could tell that she was really committing to it. And with every pass, with every scrambled sound of my hair being stripped away from me, I knew it was stripping away the armor. Everything that was safe, everything that was normal was vanishing before my eyes.

As clumps of my hair showered the floor and the first signs of the mohawk were emerging, I felt two things. The first was liberation. I'd be able to show people that I wasn't scared of letting people know I loved Green Day, Flogging Molly, Deftones, All That Remains, Mötorhead. It was more than freeing. It felt right. People didn't know this side of me—this capacity to show everyone I walk by that I am who I am. It's a bold statement, the mohawk, but that's the point, right?

The second thing I felt was: *Oh shit.*

They shave your head in the Marines, sure, but they shave all of it. They don't carve it into a spiked testament to something most people equate with anarchy. I immediately thought of all of my military brothers and what they'd think. Then, I started thinking about work. I mean, I have a freaking day job. I can't rock a mohawk at two in the afternoon and be taken seriously.

It was like a house of cards. All of these thoughts started tumbling down on me.

I hadn't even considered my parents' reactions. As cool as they'd been with everything else prior to this, they were mortified. I'll never forget their faces. I had to quietly remind them about the Halloween costumes, the road tours my dad took, the Marines. All of it. I had to remind them how they reminded *me* that it's important to step outside yourself and be bold. Do it, chase it, be it. That sort of thing.

I didn't realize how many of these values my parents instilled in me until the mohawk, believe it or not. It was an odd thing to remind *them* that they'd shaped me into a person unafraid of walking around with a mohawk.

Erin's reaction was priceless—and she was the one who dared me to do it. Maybe she didn't expect me to come back from O'Hairons in South Amherst with a fully waxed, spiked, intimidating mohawk. But when I did, I could see reality settling into her eyes.

"Oh my God," she mouthed. "You actually did it."

I could see a dozen emotions play across her face. For a few seconds, I could see awe and maybe joy, but then those emotions were quickly crushed by the waves of: "I can't go out into public with you!" and "No way in hell can you do this. Can you wear a hat?" Eventually, she settled on: "This was a hilarious joke. You called my bluff. Now grow the hair back in."

I played a gig that weekend with Poormercy and I decided to keep the mohawk. I stepped out on that stage and tuned my bass and ignored the comments. I could *feel* how people were looking at me at the time. Hell, I could feel them *looking*. I could literally feel the intensity with which people would either stare at me as well as the intensity with which people would avoid me. Both are hugely powerful and I had no idea until then.

Moreover, *I* felt different. I felt like me.

The mohawk's almost like a holstered weapon: people can see it's there but you're not flailing it around, threatening people. You have it on you for no other purpose than to keep it handy. And not really caring (or sometimes even remembering) that you have a mohawk on your fucking head?

Well, that's when you know you're you.

+

Eventually, the mohawk became a means to an end. It was supposed to be a temporary thing. The idea is that I'd dress up as a goofball and deejay for weddings and shit was not a long-term scenario. Before I knew it, I started getting gigs left and right. I even told some clients that I'd tone it down with the mohawk and they'd come back and say: "You lose the haircut, you lose the job."

I was suddenly like the centerpiece to a wedding cake.

I'm really good on a microphone and I love getting crowds of people together to do things they'd normally never do. Getting a bunch of hardcore jocks to do the Macarena or dance to "Cantaloop" is one of my all-time favorite things in the world.

Any real musician will tell you that deejays are the Antichrist when it comes to music. For someone to make money for playing other people's music—that's just distasteful.

I didn't care.

I took a funky haircut and turned it into a paying job.

We had an old pawn-shop PA and a board that Dave Brubeck himself probably started on. We were in heaven when we got it. In our heads, more power equaled more volume. It began a sound war that could be heard in a one-mile radius of the base. It was a good thing we lived with a couple hundred other like-minded jarheads who loved live music.

Who cared if it was good? It was loud.

The board was Shawn's baby and it was the beginning of the button-pushing musical mad scientist he's become. Since then, I've seen him do magic with the board. Hell, I've recorded some garbage with Shawn that made me think Vinnie Paul himself laid it down.

- Chris Cahill

"POP SONG 89"
—R.E.M.

Understand what you're getting yourself into and educate yourself. That's what anyone in a band needs to always be thinking.

You may have a band that's two weeks old but they have an opportunity to be in front of a producer or a record label and instantly have a path that a musician of twenty-five years might not. The opposite might be true, too: you might be on your last leg.

You need to understand that it all happens for a reason and you can't afford to have an ego about anything when it comes to being in a band.

You're always learning.

You're never taking anything for granted.

You're never forgetting what's happened but you're also not *not* looking forward.

Music rarely looks backward.

+

The perfect pop song is what everyone secretly wants to make. I swear to God this is true. Most everyone in the music industry will say otherwise, but they're lying. All of them. Everyone wants to follow the blueprints and create bubble-gum architecture alongside Taylor Swift and Katy Perry.

The perfect pop song isn't hard to diagram.

The intro grabs listeners' attention within the first fifteen seconds. That's crucial. If not, you've lost because you're already bringing in a chunk of the chorus right to the beginning.

It's like a bumper sticker: it's some phrase or notion that gets stuck in your head. Easy to remember. Think along the lines of an action movie trailer. You see the explosions and go: *Well, shit. Now I'm interested.*

That happens within the first fifteen seconds of a pop song. *Boom.*

The verse has to have a melody line that keeps the listener engaged. If you keep the verse nice, short, and tight at the beginning, you can sort of "tease" the listener with another taste of that chorus.

In the second verse, you'll layer in the instruments a little more thickly, a little more lusciously. There'll be more orchestration there. Again, it's all part of the plan. Subconsciously, you're still pulling the listener in.

Now we have the bridge.

That's the part of the song that ties one part to the next. In the old days, a bridge was considered as the part of a song that takes the listener on a trip, on a journey.

Truth be told, the bridge is just another chorus.

Listen to "Don't Stop Believing" by Journey. Seriously, check that one out. It's all bridges or pre-choruses. In every part of that song, the actual chorus doesn't happen until the end.

The Ramones knew how to craft a fucking song, man. Every single was under three minutes with three chords. They didn't mess around. They were so efficient. For my money, that's the epitome of purity.

It's really fast, it's not perfect, and you can't understand every lyric.[26] It's nothing you'd hear playing in the background at a white table-cloth dinner with expensive wine. (Then again, it'd be perfect dinner music for me.)

After the bridge, there's usually a little riff or a quick solo. Something that distinguishes the song a bit. A little touch, a little flourish. And if the song has an actual point or story—the good ones always do—the story gets a little deeper.

Basically, if you're writing a great pop song, all you're doing is setting it up so that the next chorus blows your fucking doors off.

That's it.

It's all a lesson in ascension, raising the stakes, and delivering on your promise.

---

[26] Similar sentiments could be said about this book.

+

There are techniques producers use in the studio that are tried-and-true. Old as sin, but they get results.

There are ways to prepare singers, or to motivate them psychologically in the studio. There are tricks in changing one little guitar part that will completely change the entire song. A key change; a shift from a minor to a major. It makes all the difference.

Maybe you'll have a vocalist sing a song as if out of breath, so you'll have them run around the room and do jumping jacks, then immediately get on the mike. The context of a song could be about losing all my energy, being stressed, losing your mind, and with the vocalist being out of breath, it adds that extra element to the music.

Producers' jobs are to add reality, heart, and honesty to someone else's music.

Nothing else.

This is, of course, ironic since pop music is fundamentally all artifice, but my job as a producer is to give it some semblance of credibility.

We're the ones making sure that you don't see the strings, don't notice the curtain, nor see beyond the smoke and mirrors.

When I first met Shawn during a bachelor party, he stood out. He had a large mohawk. Were it a group of people that had mohawks, it wouldn't have stood out quite so much. But he was the <u>only</u> person with a mohawk. And he wore sunglasses in a limousine. But he greeted me with a warm and hearty handshake, and I knew we'd be Facebook friends before the end of the night.

I think, during the course of the night, we went to a bar with dancing ladies, but we weren't allowed in that bar. Perhaps we exuded radioactivity (from the wings and bread we ate for dinner) or maybe they were full-up with pant-jangling dudes. I guess we'll never know. But I think the door guy at the dancing-ladies place saw Shawn and said "No, way. This guy's got a groin that won't stop and he's going to bust through all of our ladies. They won't be able to dance!"

I think that's what happened at least…

- Chris Barber

"GOT ME WRONG"
—Alice in Chains

I don't ever care if anyone has a past. I don't consciously absorb information that people may have told me about you. I never have a predisposition about you like: "Hey, that dude's an asshole. Don't talk to him."[27]

That never, ever registers with me.

I treat people by the Golden Rule, brother. If you look at this "thing" on top my head, if I got judged every day of the week—I wouldn't leave the house. I've been that way all my life. I try to find a common ground with everybody.

We can always find that.

---

[27] There are very few exceptions, but there are a couple. Trust me. You know who you are.

I once worked with Steve Albini on an album. He's a legendary producer[28] who's worked with everyone from Nirvana to Joanna Newsom to Veruca Salt to Cloud Nothings. The dude is legit. I walked right into his studio in Chicago with my mohawk standing proud. He admired it (as much as Steve Albini admires anything) and I'm sure it's because he embraces noisy rebellion.

He didn't flinch when he saw me. He found the common ground.

But not everyone is Steve Albini.

Most days of the week, I have to worry about the mohawk.

I have to hide it.

I routinely walk into council chambers and I meet with mayors. Walking in with a twelve-inch mohawk on my head isn't going to convince anyone that I'm the most responsible person in the world.

So I slick my hair back, put on a golf cap, and turn into Clark Kent. I dress that part, complete with buttoned-up shirts that I iron every morning, thick-rimmed glasses, and a golf cap.

---

[28] He's the type of guy who would absolutely loathe this description.

That's my costume.

And I honestly don't mind playing that part.

There's a scene in that Western *Young Guns II* where they arrest Billy the Kid. Now, I'm not saying I'm Billy the Kid or anything. (I'm not saying I'm legendary, either. Please know that.) But after they arrest him, in the next scene, he's doing gun tricks for the governor and vice governor. They're all sitting there and admiring him.

That's what I see happening when the people I work with see this book.

It'll go from: "Oh shit, you're going to kill me?" to "That's right. I worked with Steve Albini on an album. You want to hear some punk rock I used to play in Hawaii?"

+

I'll open a newspaper and read about some drug bust in towns near Milan: Norwalk, Sandusky, Monroeville. The guy who's arrested will be my age. I always wonder what they were like twenty years ago when I was getting into the music I was listening to, when I was just starting to learn the bass, when I was just figuring out my place in the world.

Or trying to.

I wonder what music they were listening to, what their plans for the future were.

After all, where you are right now is not where you will be for the rest of your life. It's just where you are on the way to somewhere else.

+

I love those who judge me before getting to know me. That wasn't always the case, but now it is. They try to make me a negative example of something, or say something about me in the presence of others to make me feel bad about myself and my decisions in life.

Maybe they just want to get a reaction out of me.

I'll usually approach them with a handshake and a smile, which completely takes them off- guard. It's like they're waiting for me to punch them in the face or talk about overthrowing the system. Power to the people. Shit like that.

That's happened everywhere from my deejaying gigs to weddings. People see the mohawk and think I'm either a.) an anarchist; b.) going bald; or c.) worthless.

By the end of the night, they've usually become my biggest fans.

+

I'm really proud of the good things in my life. I don't feel good about the bad things.

I know that doesn't sound profound at all, but it is to me.

Without the bad things, I wouldn't be doing what I'm doing now: running my own music studio and working with bands hungry to make a name for themselves, all while creating and shaping music that lives and breathes and evolves in my house. I also wouldn't be married to my wife. I wouldn't have the friends that I have. I wouldn't be happy—and, more importantly, understand what true happiness is.

The mohawk is my reminder of that.

"WE ARE NEVER EVER GETTING BACK TOGETHER"
—Taylor Swift

1. None of the Above
2. Plastic Cat
3. Six-Pack Race Track
4. Scapegoat
5. Jesus Chrysler Supercar
6. 60-Cycle Hum
7. Asphalt Junkies
8. Ballistic Hedgehog
9. Bark Spackle
10. Beat Me Please

11. Blood on Blonde
12. Outcome Input
13. Unlimited Edition
14. We Drive Fire
15. The Stick-Up Kids
16. Helen Keller Plaid
17. Poultry in Motion
18. Willie Nelson Mandela
19. Do The Math
20. Girth
21. The Fighting Hellfish
22. Smoke Yourself Thin
23. Snuffleupagus
24. Terror Firma
25. Avengalism
26. Banana Buzzkill
27. Tastes Like Chicken
28. Jehovah's Witness Protection Program
29. John Cougar Concentration Camp
30. The Joint Chiefs
31. Hillbilly Idol
32. The Fat Chick from Wilson Phillips
33. Jonestown Punch
34. Not Without My Camel
35. Shirley Temple of Doom
36. The Stabtown Assassins
37. Porno Ricans
38. Donkey Punch Bunch
39. JFKFC
40. Kathleen Turner Overdrive
41. Gringo Starr[29]

---

[29] This would be a mariachi band tribute to The Beatles. Juan Lennon, Pablo McCarthy, Jorge Harrison, and Gringo Starr.

42. Bruised Taint
43. Hot Box
44. Short Bus[30]
45. You and Your Damned Knick-Knacks
46. Captain Obvious
47. The Absinthe Ballot
48. Purple Herbie
49. Poormercy[31]
50. Buffalo Junk
51. The Brady Bunch Lawnmower Massacre
52. Dan Rather Not
53. Full-Tilt Spock
54. Underdog[32]
55. Black Dune Cat[33]
56. 33-Inch Mickeys[34]
57. Jewish Sex Wax[35]
58. Swinging Udders
59. Big in Japan
60. Spark[36]
61. REO Speed-dealer
62. Pelvic Promenade
63. Screaming Yeast Demons
64. Amber's Ashes[37]
65. Devine[38]
66. Cóiste Bodhar
67. System of a Down Syndrome

---

[30] Real band: Paul Fuhr, Steve Lener, me
[31] Real band: Sean Steffanni, Allan Carder, Jim Parker, me
[32] Real band: Todd Cavello, Sean Steffanni, Jim Slushman, me
[33] Real band: Mike Swisher, Kaz, Chris Cahill, me
[34] Real band: Scott Kalous, Cahill, Jeff Moody, me
[35] Real band: Tom Schenk, Jon Caskey, Steve Lener, Mike Prout, me
[36] Real band: Matt Raymond, Phil Weilnau, Mike Prout, Steve Lener, Brad Bailey, Dan Haas
[37] Real band: Cahill, Cory Simo, Chris Morgan, Corey Franks, me
[38] Real band: Cahill, Simo, Kim Acoustic, Shawn Nize, Tony Kordish, me

68. The Hold Still
69. Laugh Track
70. Sound Travels
71. Dumbass Blonde
72. Life Alert The Shades
73. We Are Giving You Gold!
74. Prison Bitch
75. Sara Bellum
76. Whereabouts
77. A Violet Mind
78. Stranger Danger
79. The Lunchbox Heroes
80. The Punky Brewsters
81. The Mike Hockout Band
82. Polonium 210
83. Blanket Party
84. American Short Stories
85. Keanu Whoa
86. Zero Down
87. For All of August
88. Due North
89. Wishcraft
90. Gag Reflex
91. The Anonymous Party
92. Half a Chance
93. Radio Baghdad
94. Killer Rabbit
95. Poop Shoot Riot
96. Shoot Dolores
97. Petraeus and the All-Ins
98. Not Rocket Surgery
99. F.O.C. (Friends of Charlie)
100. The End